Cram101 Textbook Outlines to accompany:

Macroeconomics

N. Gregory Mankiw, 7th Edition

Learning System

Cram101 Textbook Outlines is a learning system. The notes in this book are the highlights of your textbook, you will never have to highlight a book again.

How to use this book. Take this book to class, it is your notebook for the lecture. The notes and highlights on the left hand side of the pages follow the outline and order of the textbook. All you have to do is follow along while your instructor presents the lecture. Circle the items emphasized in class and add other important information on the right side. With Cram101 Textbook Outlines you'll spend less time writing and more time listening. Learning becomes more efficient.

Cram101.com Online

Increase your studying efficiency by using Cram101.com's practice tests and online reference material. It is the perfect complement to Cram101 Textbook Outlines. Use self-teaching matching tests or simulate in-class testing with comprehensive multiple choice tests, or simply use Cram's true and false tests for quick review. Cram101.com even allows you to enter your in-class notes for an integrated studying format combining the textbook notes with your class notes.

Visit **www.Cram101.com**, click Sign Up at the top of the screen, and enter **DK73DW15273** in the promo code box on the registration screen. Your access to www.Cram101.com is discounted by 50% because you have purchased this book. Sign up and stop highlighting textbooks forever.

 ISBN(s): 9781617446405. PUBI-5.20101215

Macroeconomics
N. Gregory Mankiw, 7th

CONTENTS

Chapter 1. The Science of Macroeconomics

Macroeconomics	Macroeconomics is a branch of economics that deals with the performance, structure, behavior and decision-making of the entire economy, be that a national, regional, or the global economy. Along with microeconomics, Macroeconomics is one of the two most general fields in economics. Macroeconomists study aggregated indicators such as GDP, unemployment rates, and price indices to understand how the whole economy functions.
Aggregate Demand-Aggregate Supply model	Aggregate Demand-Aggregate Supply model is a macroeconomic model that explains price level and output through the relationship of aggregate demand and aggregate supply. It was first put forth by John Maynard Keynes in his work The General Theory of Employment, Interest, and Money. It is the foundation for the modern field of macroeconomics, and is accepted by a broad array of economists, from Libertarian, Monetarist supporters of laissez-faire, such as Milton Friedman to Socialist, Post-Keynesian supporters of economic interventionism, such as Joan Robinson.
Bretton Woods system	The Bretton Woods system is commonly understood to refer to the international monetary regime that prevailed from the end of World War II until the early 1970s. Taking its name from the site of the 1944 conference that created the International Monetary Fund (IMF) and World Bank, the Bretton Woods system was history`s first example of a fully negotiated monetary order intended to govern currency relations among sovereign states. In principle, the regime was designed to combine binding legal obligations with multilateral decision-making conducted through an international organization, the IMF, endowed with limited supranational authority.
Deflation	Deflation is a decrease in the general price level of goods and services. Deflation occurs when the annual inflation rate falls below zero percent (a negative inflation rate), resulting in an increase in the real value of money - allowing one to buy more goods with the same amount of money. This should not be confused with disinflation, a slow-down in the inflation rate.
Federal Open Market Committee	The Federal Open Market Committee a component of the Federal Reserve System, is charged under United States law with overseeing the nation`s open market operations. It is the Federal Reserve committee that makes key decisions about interest rates and the growth of the United States money supply. It is the principal organ of United States national monetary policy.
Real gross domestic product	Real gross domestic product is a macroeconomic measure of the size of an economy adjusted for price changes Gross domestic product is defined as the market value of all final goods and services produced in a geographical region, usually a country. That market value depends on two things: the actual quantity of goods and services produced, and their price. The actual quantity of goods and services produced is sometimes called the volume.

Chapter 1. The Science of Macroeconomics

Government debt	Government debt is money (or credit) owed by any level of government; either central government, federal government, municipal government or local government. By contrast, annual government deficit refers to the difference between government receipts and spending in a single year. Debt of a sovereign government is called sovereign debt.
Hyperinflation	Hyperinflation is inflation that is very high or `out of control`, a condition in which prices increase rapidly as a currency loses its value. Definitions used by the media vary from a cumulative inflation rate over three years approaching 100% to `inflation exceeding 50% a month.` In informal usage the term is often applied to much lower rates. As a rule of thumb, normal inflation is reported per year, but Hyperinflation is often reported for much shorter intervals, often per month.
Normal goods	In economics, Normal goods are any goods for which demand increases when income increases and falls when income decreases but price remains constant, i.e. with a positive income elasticity of demand. The term does not necessarily refer to the quality of the good. Depending on the indifference curves, the amount of a good bought can either increase, decrease, or stay the same when income increases.
Recession	In economics, a Recession is a business cycle contraction, a general slowdown in economic activity over a period of time. During Recessions, many macroeconomic indicators vary in a similar way. Production as measured by Gross Domestic Product (GDP), employment, investment spending, capacity utilization, household incomes, business profits and inflation all fall during Recessions; while bankruptcies and the unemployment rate rise.
Tax cut	Economic stimulus via Tax cuts, along with interest rate intervention and deficit spending, are one of the central tenets of Keynesian economics. The immediate effects of a Tax cut are, generally, a decrease in the real income of the government and an increase in the real income of those whose tax rate has been lowered.
Budget deficit	A budget deficit occurs when an entity spends more money than it takes in. The opposite of a budget deficit is a budget surplus.

Income	Income is the consumption and savings opportunity gained by an entity within a specified time frame, which is generally expressed in monetary terms. However, for households and individuals, \`Income is the sum of all the wages, salaries, profits, interests payments, rents and other forms of earnings received... in a given period of time.\` For firms, Income generally refers to net-profit: what remains of revenue after expenses have been subtracted.
Interest rate	An Interest rate is the price a borrower pays for the use of money they borrow from a lender, for instance a small company might borrow capital from a bank to buy new assets for their business, and the return a lender receives for deferring the use of funds, by lending it to the borrower. Interests rates are fundamental to a capitalist society. Interest rates are normally expressed as a percentage rate over the period of one year.
Investment	Investment is the commitment of money or capital to purchase financial instruments or other assets in order to gain profitable returns in form of interest, income, or appreciation of the value of the instrument. It is related to saving or deferring consumption. Investment is involved in many areas of the economy, such as business management and finance no matter for households, firms, or governments.
Money	Money is anything that is generally accepted as payment for goods and services and repayment of debts. The main functions of Money are distinguished as: a medium of exchange; a unit of account; a store of value; and, occasionally, a standard of deferred payment. Money originated as commodity Money, but nearly all contemporary Money systems are based on fiat Money.
Nominal interest rate	In finance and economics Nominal interest rate refers to the rate of interest before adjustment for inflation (in contrast with the real interest rate); or, for interest rates \`as stated\` without adjustment for the full effect of compounding (also referred to as the nominal annual rate). An interest rate is called nominal if the frequency of compounding (e.g. a month) is not identical to the basic time unit (normally a year).
Population growth	In demography, Population growth is used informally for the more specific term Population growth rate , and is often used to refer specifically to the growth of the human population of the world. Simple models of Population growth include the Malthusian Growth Model and the logistic model.

In demographics and ecology, Population growth rate (PGR) is the fractional rate at which the number of individuals in a population increases.

Stagflation

In economics, the term Stagflation refers to the situation when both the inflation rate and the unemployment rate are high. It is a difficult economic condition for a country, as both inflation and economic stagnation occur simultaneously and no macroeconomic policy can address both of these problems at the same time.

The portmanteau Stagflation is generally attributed to British politician Iain Macleod, who coined the term in a speech to Parliament in 1965.

Standard of living

Standard of living is generally measured by standards such as real (i.e. inflation adjusted) income per person and poverty rate. Other measures such as access and quality of health care, income growth inequality and educational standards are also used. Examples are access to certain goods , or measures of health such as life expectancy.

Surplus

The term surplus is used in economics for several related quantities. The consumer surplus is the amount that consumers benefit by being able to purchase a product for a price that is less than the most that they would be willing to pay. The producer surplus is the amount that producers benefit by selling at a market price mechanism that is higher than the least that they would be willing to sell for.

Depression

In economics, a depression is a sustained, long-term downturn in economic activity in one or more economies. It is a more severe downturn than a recession, which is seen by economists as part of a normal business cycle.

Considered a rare and extreme form of recession, a depression is characterized by its length, and by abnormally large increases in unemployment, falls in the availability of credit-- quite often due to some kind of banking/financial crisis, shrinking output and investment, numerous bankruptcies-- including sovereign debt defaults, significantly reduced amounts of trade and commerce-- especially international, as well as highly volatile relative currency value fluctuations-- most often due to devaluations.

Inflation	In economics, Inflation is a rise in the general level of prices of goods and services in an economy over a period of time. When the price level rises, each unit of currency buys fewer goods and services; consequently, annual Inflation is also an erosion in the purchasing power of money - a loss of real value in the internal medium of exchange and unit of account in the economy. A chief measure of price Inflation is the Inflation rate, the annualized percentage change in a general price index over time.
Inflation rate	In economics, the Inflation rate is a measure of inflation, the rate of increase of a price index . It is the percentage rate of change in price level over time. The rate of decrease in the purchasing power of money is approximately equal. The Inflation rate is used to calculate the real interest rate, as well as real increases in wages, and official measurements of this rate act as input variables to COLA adjustments and inflation derivatives prices.
Great Depression	The Great Depression was a severe worldwide economic depression in the decade preceding World War II. The timing of the Great Depression varied across nations, but in most countries it started in about 1929 and lasted until the late 1930s or early 1940s. It was the longest, most widespread, and deepest depression of the 20th century, and is used in the 21st century as an example of how far the world`s economy can decline.
Economic model	In economics, a model is a theoretical construct that represents economic processes by a set of variables and a set of logical and/or quantitative relationships between them. The Economic model is a simplified framework designed to illustrate complex processes, often but not always using mathematical techniques. Frequently, Economic models use structural parameters.
Consumer price index	A Consumer price index is a measure estimating the average price of consumer goods and services purchased by households. A Consumer price index measures a price change for a constant market basket of goods and services from one period to the next within the same area (city, region, or nation). It is a price index determined by measuring the price of a standard group of goods meant to represent the typical market basket of a typical urban consumer.
Market clearing	In economics, Market clearing refers to either · a simplifying assumption made by the new classical school that markets always go to where the quantity supplied equals the quantity demanded; or · the process of getting there via price adjustment A Market clearing price is the price of goods or a service at which quantity supplied is equal to quantity demanded. Also called the equilibrium price.

In simple terms, this means that markets tend to move towards prices which balance the quantity supplied and the quantity demanded, such that the market will eventually be cleared of all surpluses and shortages (excess supply and demand).

Microeconomics

Microeconomics is a branch of economics that studies how the individual parts of the economy, the household and the firms, make decisions to allocate limited resources, typically in markets where goods or services are being bought and sold. Microeconomics examines how these decisions and behaviours affect the supply and demand for goods and services, which determines prices, and how prices, in turn, determine the supply and demand of goods and services.

This is a contrast to macroeconomics, which involves the `sum total of economic activity, dealing with the issues of growth, inflation, and unemployment.

Utility

In economics, Utility is a measure of relative satisfaction. Given this measure, one may speak meaningfully of increasing or decreasing Utility, and thereby explain economic behavior in terms of attempts to increase one`s Utility. Utility is often modeled to be affected by consumption of various goods and services, possession of wealth and spending of leisure time.

Aggregate demand

In macroeconomics, Aggregate demand is the total demand for final goods and services in the economy (Y) at a given time and price level. It is the amount of goods and services in the economy that will be purchased at all possible price levels. This is the demand for the gross domestic product of a country when inventory levels are static.

Aggregate supply

In economics, Aggregate supply is the total supply of goods and services that firms in a national economy plan on selling during a specific time period. It is the total amount of goods and services that firms are willing to sell at a given price level in an economy.

In neo-Keynesian theory seen in many textbooks, an `Aggregate supply and demand` diagram is drawn that looks like a typical Marshallian supply and demand diagram.

James Tobin

James Tobin was an American economist who in his lifetime, had served on the Council of Economic Advisors, the Board of Governors of the Federal Reserve System, and had taught at Harvard and Yale Universities. He developed the ideas of Keynesian economics, and advocated government intervention to stabilize output and avoid recessions. His academic work included pioneering contributions to the study of investment, monetary and fiscal policy and financial markets.

Chapter 2. The Data of Macroeconomics

Bureau of Economic Analysis	The Bureau of Economic Analysis is an agency in the United States Department of Commerce that provides important economic statistics including the gross domestic product of the United States. Its stated mission is to `promote a better understanding of the U.S. economy by providing the most timely, relevant, and accurate economic data in an objective and cost-effective manner`.
Circular flow of income	In neoclassical economics, the terms Circular flow of income refer to a simple economic model which describes the reciprocal circulation of income between producers and consumers. In the circular flow model, the inter-dependent entities of producer and consumer are referred to as `firms` and `households` respectively and provide each other with factors in order to facilitate the flow of income. Firms provide consumers with goods and services in exchange for consumer expenditure and `factors of production` from households.
Consumption	Consumption is a common concept in economics, and gives rise to derived concepts such as consumer debt. Generally, Consumption is defined in part by opposition to production. But the precise definition can vary because different schools of economists define production quite differently.
Real gross domestic product	Real gross domestic product is a macroeconomic measure of the size of an economy adjusted for price changes Gross domestic product is defined as the market value of all final goods and services produced in a geographical region, usually a country. That market value depends on two things: the actual quantity of goods and services produced, and their price. The actual quantity of goods and services produced is sometimes called the volume.
GDP deflator	In economics, the GDP deflator is a measure of the level of prices of all new, domestically produced, final goods and services in an economy. GDP stands for gross domestic product, the total value of all final goods and services produced within that economy during a specified period. In most systems of national accounts the GDP deflator measures the ratio of nominal (or current-price) GDP to the real (or chain volume) measure of GDP. The formula used to calculate the deflator is: $\text{GDP deflator} = \frac{\text{Nominal GDP}}{\text{Real GDP}} \times 100$

	Dividing the nominal GDP by the GDP deflator and multiplying it by 100 would then give the figure for real GDP, hence deflating the nominal GDP into a real measure.
Gross domestic product	The Gross domestic product or gross domestic income (GDI) is a measure of a country`s overall economic output. It is the market value of all final goods and services made within the borders of a country in a year. It is often positively correlated with the standard of living,; though its use as a stand-in for measuring the standard of living has come under increasing criticism and many countries are actively exploring alternative measures to Gross domestic product for that purpose.
Income	Income is the consumption and savings opportunity gained by an entity within a specified time frame, which is generally expressed in monetary terms. However, for households and individuals, `Income is the sum of all the wages, salaries, profits, interests payments, rents and other forms of earnings received... in a given period of time.` For firms, Income generally refers to net-profit: what remains of revenue after expenses have been subtracted.
Investment	Investment is the commitment of money or capital to purchase financial instruments or other assets in order to gain profitable returns in form of interest, income, or appreciation of the value of the instrument. It is related to saving or deferring consumption. Investment is involved in many areas of the economy, such as business management and finance no matter for households, firms, or governments.
Balance of trade	The Balance of trade is the difference between the monetary value of exports and imports of output in an economy over a certain period. It is the relationship between a nation`s imports and exports. A positive or favorable Balance of trade is known as a trade surplus if it consists of exporting more than is imported; a negative or unfavorable balance is referred to as a trade deficit or, informally, a trade gap. The Balance of trade is sometimes divided into a goods and a services balance.
Stock	The Stock or capital Stock of a business entity represents the original capital paid into or invested in the business by its founders. It serves as a security for the creditors of a business since it cannot be withdrawn to the detriment of the creditors. Stock is distinct from the property and the assets of a business which may fluctuate in quantity and value.
Good	In economics and accounting, a good is physical product that can be used to satisfy some desire or need. It can be contrasted with a service which is intangible, whereas a good is a tangible physical product, capable of being delivered to a purchaser and involves the transfer of ownership from seller to customer. For example, an apple is a tangible good, as opposed to a haircut, which is an (intangible) service.

Goods and services	In economics, economic output is divided into physical goods and intangible services. Consumption of Goods and services is assumed to produce utility. It is often used when referring to a Goods and services Tax.
Aggregate demand	In macroeconomics, Aggregate demand is the total demand for final goods and services in the economy (Y) at a given time and price level. It is the amount of goods and services in the economy that will be purchased at all possible price levels. This is the demand for the gross domestic product of a country when inventory levels are static.
Population growth	In demography, Population growth is used informally for the more specific term Population growth rate , and is often used to refer specifically to the growth of the human population of the world. Simple models of Population growth include the Malthusian Growth Model and the logistic model. In demographics and ecology, Population growth rate (PGR) is the fractional rate at which the number of individuals in a population increases.
Intermediate goods	Intermediate goods or producer goods are goods used as inputs in the production of other goods, such as partly finished goods. They are goods used in production of final goods. A firm may make then use Intermediate goods, or make then sell, or buy then use them.
Value added	In economics, the difference between the sale price of a product and the cost of materials to produce it is the Value added. In national accounts used in macroeconomics, it refers to the contribution of the factors of production, i.e., land, labour, and capital goods, to raising the value of a product and corresponds to the incomes received by the owners of these factors. The national Value added is shared between capital and labor , and this sharing gives rise to issues of distribution.
Exchange	An exchange is a highly organized market where (especially) tradable securities, commodities, foreign exchange, futures, and options contracts are sold and bought. exchanges bring together brokers and dealers who buy and sell these objects. These various financial instruments can typically be sold either through the exchange, typically with the benefit of a clearinghouse to cover defaults, or over-the-counter, where there is typically less protection against counterparty risk from clearinghouses although OTC clearinghouses have become more common over the years, with regulators placing pressure on the OTC markets to clear and display trades openly.

Exchange rate

In finance, the Exchange rates between two currencies specifies how much one currency is worth in terms of the other. It is the value of a foreign nation`s currency in terms of the home nation`s currency.

Mundell-Fleming model

The Mundell-Fleming model is an economic model first set forth by Robert Mundell and Marcus Fleming. The model is an extension of the IS-LM model. Whereas the traditional IS-LM Model deals with economy under autarky (or a closed economy), the Mundell-Fleming model tries to describe an open economy.

Capital

In economics, capital, capital goods, or real capital are factors of production used to create goods or services that are not themselves significantly consumed (though they may depreciate) in the production process. capital goods may be acquired with money or financial capital.

In finance and accounting, capital generally refers to saved-up financial wealth, especially that used to start or maintain a business.

Percentage change

A Percentage change is a way to express a change in a variable. It represents the relative change between the old value and the new one.

For example, if a house today is worth $100,000 and the year after its worth goes up to $110,000, the Percentage change of its worth can be expressed as

$$\frac{110000 - 100000}{100000} = 0.1 = 10\%.$$

It can then be said that the worth of the house went up by 10%.

Security

A security is a fungible, negotiable instrument representing financial value. Securities are broadly categorized into debt securities (such as banknotes, bonds and debentures) and equity securities, e.g., common stocks; and derivative contracts, such as forwards, futures, options and swaps. The company or other entity issuing the security is called the issuer.

Social Security

Social security is primarily a social insurance program providing social protection, or protection against socially recognized conditions, including poverty, old age, disability, unemployment and others. Social security may refer to:

· social insurance, where people receive benefits or services in recognition of contributions to an insurance scheme. These services typically include provision for retirement pensions, disability insurance, survivor benefits and unemployment insurance.

· income maintenance--mainly the distribution of cash in the event of interruption of employment, including retirement, disability and unemployment

· services provided by administrations responsible for Social security. In different countries this may include medical care, aspects of social work and even industrial relations.

· More rarely, the term is also used to refer to basic security, a term roughly equivalent to access to basic necessities--things such as food, clothing, shelter, education, money, and medical care.

Transfer payment

In economics, a Transfer payment is a redistribution of income in the market system. These payments are considered to be nonexhaustive because they do not directly absorb resources or create output. Examples of certain Transfer payments include welfare (financial aid), social security, and government subsidies for certain businesses (firms).

Consumption of fixed capital

Consumption of fixed capital is a term used in business accounts, tax assessments and national accounts for depreciation of fixed assets. CFC is used in preference to `depreciation` to emphasize that fixed capital is used up in the process of generating new output, and because unlike depreciation it is not valued at historic cost; CFC may include other expenses incurred in using or installing fixed assets beyond actual depreciation charges. Normally the term applies only to producing enterprises, but sometimes it applies also to real estate assets.

Net national product

Net national product is the total market value of all final goods and services produced by residents in a country or other polity during a given period minus depreciation. The net domestic product (NDP) is the equivalent application of Net national product within macroeconomics, and NDP is equal to gross domestic product (GDP) minus depreciation: NDP = GDP - depreciation.

Depreciation (also known as consumption of fixed capital) measures the amount of GNP that must be spent on new capital goods to maintain the existing physical capital stock.

Personal income

In economics, Personal Income refers to an individual`s total earnings from wages, investment enterprises, and other ventures.

Seasonal adjustment

Seasonal adjustment is a statistical method for removing the seasonal component of a time series used when analyzing non-seasonal trends.

The investigation of many economic time series becomes problematic due to seasonal fluctuations. Series are made up of four components:

S_t: The Seasonal Component

T_t: The Trend Component

C_t: The Cyclical Component

I_t: The Error, or irregular component.

Bureau of Labor Statistics

The Bureau of Labor Statistics is a unit of the United States Department of Labor. It is the principal fact-finding agency for the U.S. government in the broad field of labor economics and statistics. The BLS is a governmental statistical agency that collects, processes, analyzes, and disseminates essential statistical data to the American public, the U.S. Congress, other Federal agencies, State and local governments, business, and labor representatives.

Consumer price index

A Consumer price index is a measure estimating the average price of consumer goods and services purchased by households. A Consumer price index measures a price change for a constant market basket of goods and services from one period to the next within the same area (city, region, or nation). It is a price index determined by measuring the price of a standard group of goods meant to represent the typical market basket of a typical urban consumer.

Aggregate Demand-Aggregate Supply model	Aggregate Demand-Aggregate Supply model is a macroeconomic model that explains price level and output through the relationship of aggregate demand and aggregate supply. It was first put forth by John Maynard Keynes in his work The General Theory of Employment, Interest, and Money. It is the foundation for the modern field of macroeconomics, and is accepted by a broad array of economists, from Libertarian, Monetarist supporters of laissez-faire, such as Milton Friedman to Socialist, Post-Keynesian supporters of economic interventionism, such as Joan Robinson.
Core inflation	Core inflation is a measure of inflation which excludes certain items that face volatile price movements, notably food and energy. The preferred measure by the Federal Reserve of Core inflation in the United States is the core Personal consumption expenditures price index (PCE). This is based on chained dollars.
Deflation	Deflation is a decrease in the general price level of goods and services. Deflation occurs when the annual inflation rate falls below zero percent (a negative inflation rate), resulting in an increase in the real value of money - allowing one to buy more goods with the same amount of money. This should not be confused with disinflation, a slow-down in the inflation rate.
Hyperinflation	Hyperinflation is inflation that is very high or `out of control`, a condition in which prices increase rapidly as a currency loses its value. Definitions used by the media vary from a cumulative inflation rate over three years approaching 100% to `inflation exceeding 50% a month.` In informal usage the term is often applied to much lower rates. As a rule of thumb, normal inflation is reported per year, but Hyperinflation is often reported for much shorter intervals, often per month.
Central Bank	A Central bank, reserve bank, or monetary authority is a banking institution granted the exclusive privilege to lend a government its currency. Like a normal commercial bank, a Central bank charges interest on the loans made to borrowers, primarily the government of whichever country the bank exists for, and to other commercial banks, typically as a `lender of last resort`. However, a Central bank is distinguished from a normal commercial bank because it has a monopoly on creating the currency of that nation, which is loaned to the government in the form of legal tender.
Monetary policy	Monetary policy is the process by which the central bank or monetary authority of a country controls the supply of money and the rate of interest. Monetary policy is usually used to attain a set of objectives oriented towards the growth and stability of the economy. These goals usually include stable prices and low unemployment.

Substitution bias	Substitution bias describes a bias in economics index numbers arising from tendency to purchase inexpensive substitutes for expensive items when prices change. Substitution bias occurs when two or more items experience a change of price relative to each other. Consumers will consume more of the now comparatively inexpensive good and less of the now relatively more expensive good.
Money	Money is anything that is generally accepted as payment for goods and services and repayment of debts. The main functions of Money are distinguished as: a medium of exchange; a unit of account; a store of value; and, occasionally, a standard of deferred payment. Money originated as commodity Money, but nearly all contemporary Money systems are based on fiat Money.
Money supply	In economics, Money supply is the total amount of money available in an economy at a particular point in time. There are several ways to define \`money,\` but standard measures usually include currency in circulation and demand deposits. Money supply data are recorded and published, usually by the government or the central bank of the country. Public and private-sector analysts have long monitored changes in Money supply because of its possible effects on the price level, inflation and the business cycle.
Current Population Survey	The Current Population Survey is a statistical survey conducted by the United States Census Bureau for the Bureau of Labor Statistics (BLS). The BLS uses the data to provide a monthly report on the Employment Situation. This report provides estimates of the number of unemployed people in the United States.
Discouraged worker	In economics, a Discouraged worker is a person of legal employment age who is not actively seeking employment. This is usually because an individual has given up looking or has had no success in finding a job, hence the term \`discouraged.\` Their belief may derive from a variety of factors including: a shortage of jobs in their locality or line of work; perceived discrimination for reasons such as age, race, sex and religion; a lack of necessary skills, training, or experience; or, a chronic illness or disability.

As a general practice, Discouraged workers, who are often classified as `marginally attached to the labor force`, `on the margins` of the labor force, or as part of `hidden unemployment`, are not considered to be part of the labor force and are thus not counted in most official unemployment rates, which influences the appearance and interpretation of unemployment statistics.

Labor force

In economics, the people in the Labor force are the suppliers of labor. The Labor force is all the nonmilitary people who are officially employed or unemployed. In 2005, the worldwide Labor force was over 3 billion people.

Circular flow of income

In neoclassical economics, the terms Circular flow of income refer to a simple economic model which describes the reciprocal circulation of income between producers and consumers. In the circular flow model, the inter-dependent entities of producer and consumer are referred to as \`firms\` and \`households\` respectively and provide each other with factors in order to facilitate the flow of income. Firms provide consumers with goods and services in exchange for consumer expenditure and \`factors of production\` from households.

Real gross domestic product

Real gross domestic product is a macroeconomic measure of the size of an economy adjusted for price changes Gross domestic product is defined as the market value of all final goods and services produced in a geographical region, usually a country. That market value depends on two things: the actual quantity of goods and services produced, and their price. The actual quantity of goods and services produced is sometimes called the volume.

GDP deflator

In economics, the GDP deflator is a measure of the level of prices of all new, domestically produced, final goods and services in an economy. GDP stands for gross domestic product, the total value of all final goods and services produced within that economy during a specified period.

In most systems of national accounts the GDP deflator measures the ratio of nominal (or current-price) GDP to the real (or chain volume) measure of GDP. The formula used to calculate the deflator is:

$$\text{GDP deflator} = \frac{\text{Nominal GDP}}{\text{Real GDP}} \times 100$$

Dividing the nominal GDP by the GDP deflator and multiplying it by 100 would then give the figure for real GDP, hence deflating the nominal GDP into a real measure.

Gross domestic product

The Gross domestic product or gross domestic income (GDI) is a measure of a country\`s overall economic output. It is the market value of all final goods and services made within the borders of a country in a year. It is often positively correlated with the standard of living,; though its use as a stand-in for measuring the standard of living has come under increasing criticism and many countries are actively exploring alternative measures to Gross domestic product for that purpose.

Budget deficit	A budget deficit occurs when an entity spends more money than it takes in. The opposite of a budget deficit is a budget surplus.
Exchange	An exchange is a highly organized market where (especially) tradable securities, commodities, foreign exchange, futures, and options contracts are sold and bought. exchanges bring together brokers and dealers who buy and sell these objects. These various financial instruments can typically be sold either through the exchange, typically with the benefit of a clearinghouse to cover defaults, or over-the-counter, where there is typically less protection against counterparty risk from clearinghouses although OTC clearinghouses have become more common over the years, with regulators placing pressure on the OTC markets to clear and display trades openly.
Exchange rate	In finance, the Exchange rates between two currencies specifies how much one currency is worth in terms of the other. It is the value of a foreign nation`s currency in terms of the home nation`s currency.
Surplus	The term surplus is used in economics for several related quantities. The consumer surplus is the amount that consumers benefit by being able to purchase a product for a price that is less than the most that they would be willing to pay. The producer surplus is the amount that producers benefit by selling at a market price mechanism that is higher than the least that they would be willing to sell for.
Capital	In economics, capital, capital goods, or real capital are factors of production used to create goods or services that are not themselves significantly consumed (though they may depreciate) in the production process. capital goods may be acquired with money or financial capital. In finance and accounting, capital generally refers to saved-up financial wealth, especially that used to start or maintain a business.
Consumption	Consumption is a common concept in economics, and gives rise to derived concepts such as consumer debt. Generally, Consumption is defined in part by opposition to production. But the precise definition can vary because different schools of economists define production quite differently.

Export-oriented industrialization	Export-oriented industrialization is a trade and economic policy aiming to speed-up the industrialization process of a country through exporting goods for which the nation has a comparative advantage. Export-led growth implies opening domestic markets to foreign competition in exchange for market access in other countries, though this may not be true of all domestic markets as governments aim to protect specific nascent industries so they grow and are able to exploit their future comparative advantage and in practise the converse can occur, for example many East Asian countries had strong barriers on imports during most of the 1960s-1980s. Reduced tariff barriers, floating exchange rate (devaluation of national currency is often employed to facilitate exports), and government support for exporting sectors are all an example of policies adopted to promote Export oriented industrialization, and ultimately economic development.
Factors of production	In economics, Factors of production are the resources employed to produce goods and services. They facilitate production but do not become part of the product (as with raw materials) or become significantly transformed by the production process . To 19th century economists, the Factors of production were land (natural resources, gifts from nature), labor (the ability to work), capital goods (human-made tools and equipment) and enterprise.
Investment	Investment is the commitment of money or capital to purchase financial instruments or other assets in order to gain profitable returns in form of interest, income, or appreciation of the value of the instrument. It is related to saving or deferring consumption. Investment is involved in many areas of the economy, such as business management and finance no matter for households, firms, or governments.
Balance of trade	The Balance of trade is the difference between the monetary value of exports and imports of output in an economy over a certain period. It is the relationship between a nation`s imports and exports. A positive or favorable Balance of trade is known as a trade surplus if it consists of exporting more than is imported; a negative or unfavorable balance is referred to as a trade deficit or, informally, a trade gap. The Balance of trade is sometimes divided into a goods and a services balance.
Determinant	In algebra, the Determinant is a special number associated with any square matrix. The fundamental geometric meaning of a Determinant is a scale factor for measure when the matrix is regarded as a linear transformation. Thus a 2×2 matrix with Determinant 2 when applied to a set of points with finite area will transform those points into a set with twice the area.

Aggregate supply

In economics, Aggregate supply is the total supply of goods and services that firms in a national economy plan on selling during a specific time period. It is the total amount of goods and services that firms are willing to sell at a given price level in an economy.

In neo-Keynesian theory seen in many textbooks, an `Aggregate supply and demand` diagram is drawn that looks like a typical Marshallian supply and demand diagram.

Good

In economics and accounting, a good is physical product that can be used to satisfy some desire or need. It can be contrasted with a service which is intangible, whereas a good is a tangible physical product, capable of being delivered to a purchaser and involves the transfer of ownership from seller to customer. For example, an apple is a tangible good, as opposed to a haircut, which is an (intangible) service.

Goods and services

In economics, economic output is divided into physical goods and intangible services. Consumption of Goods and services is assumed to produce utility. It is often used when referring to a Goods and services Tax.

Production function

In microeconomics and macroeconomics, a Production function is a function that specifies the output of a firm, an industry, or an entire economy for all combinations of inputs. This function is an assumed technological relationship, based on the current state of engineering knowledge; it does not represent the result of economic choices, but rather is an externally given entity that influences economic decision-making. Almost all economic theories presuppose a Production function, either on the firm level or the aggregate level.

Returns to scale

In economics, Returns to scale and economies of scale are related terms that describe what happens as the scale of production increases in the long run, when all input levels including physical capital usage are variable (chosen by the firm). They are different terms and should not be used interchangeably.

The term Returns to scale arises in the context of a firm`s production function. It refers to changes in output resulting from a proportional change in all inputs (where all inputs increase by a constant factor). If output increases by that same proportional change then there are constant Returns to scale. If output increases by less than that proportional change, there are decreasing Returns to scale.

Aggregate demand	In macroeconomics, Aggregate demand is the total demand for final goods and services in the economy (Y) at a given time and price level. It is the amount of goods and services in the economy that will be purchased at all possible price levels. This is the demand for the gross domestic product of a country when inventory levels are static.
Consumer price index	A Consumer price index is a measure estimating the average price of consumer goods and services purchased by households. A Consumer price index measures a price change for a constant market basket of goods and services from one period to the next within the same area (city, region, or nation). It is a price index determined by measuring the price of a standard group of goods meant to represent the typical market basket of a typical urban consumer.
Deflation	Deflation is a decrease in the general price level of goods and services. Deflation occurs when the annual inflation rate falls below zero percent (a negative inflation rate), resulting in an increase in the real value of money - allowing one to buy more goods with the same amount of money. This should not be confused with disinflation, a slow-down in the inflation rate.
Factor price	In economic theory, the price of a finished item affects the factors of production, the various costs and incentives of producing it, so as to `attract` it toward a theoretical Factor price. In other words it is the concept that the price of an item tends to approach the cost of producing it. There has been much debate as to what determines Factor prices.
Hyperinflation	Hyperinflation is inflation that is very high or `out of control`, a condition in which prices increase rapidly as a currency loses its value. Definitions used by the media vary from a cumulative inflation rate over three years approaching 100% to `inflation exceeding 50% a month.` In informal usage the term is often applied to much lower rates. As a rule of thumb, normal inflation is reported per year, but Hyperinflation is often reported for much shorter intervals, often per month.
Inflation	In economics, Inflation is a rise in the general level of prices of goods and services in an economy over a period of time. When the price level rises, each unit of currency buys fewer goods and services; consequently, annual Inflation is also an erosion in the purchasing power of money - a loss of real value in the internal medium of exchange and unit of account in the economy. A chief measure of price Inflation is the Inflation rate, the annualized percentage change in a general price index over time.

Income	Income is the consumption and savings opportunity gained by an entity within a specified time frame, which is generally expressed in monetary terms. However, for households and individuals, `Income is the sum of all the wages, salaries, profits, interests payments, rents and other forms of earnings received... in a given period of time.` For firms, Income generally refers to net-profit: what remains of revenue after expenses have been subtracted.
Income distribution	In economics, Income distribution is how a nation`s total economy is distributed amongst its population..Income distribution has always been a central concern of economic theory and economic policy. Classical economists such as Adam Smith, Thomas Malthus and David Ricardo were mainly concerned with factor Income distribution, that is, the distribution of income between the main factors of production, land, labour and capital. Modern economists have also addressed this issue, but have been more concerned with the distribution of income across individuals and households.
Inventory investment	Inventory investment is a component of gross domestic product (GDP). What is produced in a certain country is naturally also sold eventually, but some of the goods produced in a given year may be sold in a later year rather in the year they are produced. Conversely, some of the goods sold in a given year might have been produced in an earlier year.
Fixed investment	Fixed investment in economics refers to investment in fixed capital, i.e. tangible capital goods , or to the replacement of depreciated capital goods which have been scrapped. Thus, Fixed investment is investment in physical assets such as machinery, land, buildings, installations, vehicles, or technology. Normally, a company balance sheet will state both the amount of expenditure on fixed assets during the quarter or year, and the total value of the stock of fixed assets owned.
Aggregate Demand-Aggregate Supply model	Aggregate Demand-Aggregate Supply model is a macroeconomic model that explains price level and output through the relationship of aggregate demand and aggregate supply. It was first put forth by John Maynard Keynes in his work The General Theory of Employment, Interest, and Money. It is the foundation for the modern field of macroeconomics, and is accepted by a broad array of economists, from Libertarian, Monetarist supporters of laissez-faire, such as Milton Friedman to Socialist, Post-Keynesian supporters of economic interventionism, such as Joan Robinson.

Demand	In economics, demand is the desire to own anything and the ability to pay for it and willingness to pay . The term demand signifies the ability or the willingness to buy a particular commodity at a given point of time. Economists record demand on a demand schedule and plot it on a graph as a demand curve that is usually downward sloping.
Marginal product	In economics, the Marginal product or marginal physical product is the extra output produced by one more unit of an input (for instance, the difference in output when a firm`s labour is increased from five to six units). Assuming that no other inputs to production change, the Marginal product of a given input X can be expressed as  $$\mathrm{MP} = \frac{\Delta \mathrm{Y}}{\Delta \mathrm{X}}$$  where ΔX is the change in a firm`s production inputs and ΔY is the change in quantity of production output. In neoclassical economics, this is the mathematical derivative of the production function....
Marginal product of capital	Marginal product of capital is the additional output resulting from the use of an additional unit of capital . It equals 1 divided by the Incremental Capital-Output Ratio. It is the partial derivative of the production function with respect to capital.
Real wages	The term Real wages refers to wages that have been adjusted for inflation. This term is used in contrast to nominal wages or unadjusted wages. The use of adjusted figures is used in undertaking some forms of economic analysis.
Lucas critique	The Lucas critique argues that it is naive to try to predict the effects of a change in economic policy entirely on the basis of relationships observed in historical data, especially highly aggregated historical data.

The basic idea pre-dates Lucas` contribution (related ideas are expressed as Campbell`s Law and Goodhart`s Law), but in a 1976 paper Lucas drove home the point that this simple notion invalidated policy advice based on conclusions drawn from estimated system of equation models. Because the parameters of those models were not structural, i.e. not policy-invariant, they would necessarily change whenever policy (the rules of the game) was changed. Policy conclusions based on those models would therefore potentially be misleading. This argument called into question the prevailing large-scale econometric models that lacked foundations in dynamic economic theory.

Black Death

The Black Death was one of the deadliest pandemics in human history, peaking in Europe between 1348 and 1350. It is widely thought to have been an outbreak of bubonic plague caused by the bacterium Yersinia pestis, but this view has recently been challenged. Usually thought to have started in Central Asia, it had reached the Crimea by 1346. From there, probably carried by fleas residing on the black rats that were regular passengers on merchant ships, it spread throughout the Mediterranean and Europe.

The Black Death is estimated to have killed 30% to 60% of Europe`s population, reducing the world`s population from an estimated 450 million to between 350 and 375 million in 1400. This has been seen as creating a series of religious, social and economic upheavals which had profound effects on the course of European history.

Euro

The Euro is the official currency of the Eurozone: 16 of the 27 Member States of the European Union (EU) and is the currency used by the EU institutions. The Eurozone consists of Austria, Belgium, Cyprus, Finland, France, Germany, Greece, Ireland, Italy, Luxembourg, Malta, the Netherlands, Portugal, Slovakia, Slovenia and Spain. Estonia is due to join the Eurozone on 1 January 2011.

Mundell-Fleming model

The Mundell-Fleming model is an economic model first set forth by Robert Mundell and Marcus Fleming. The model is an extension of the IS-LM model. Whereas the traditional IS-LM Model deals with economy under autarky (or a closed economy), the Mundell-Fleming model tries to describe an open economy.

Stagflation

In economics, the term Stagflation refers to the situation when both the inflation rate and the unemployment rate are high. It is a difficult economic condition for a country, as both inflation and economic stagnation occur simultaneously and no macroeconomic policy can address both of these problems at the same time.

The portmanteau Stagflation is generally attributed to British politician Iain Macleod, who coined the term in a speech to Parliament in 1965.

Labor productivity

Labor productivity is the amount of goods and services that a labourer produces in a given amount of time. It is one of several types of productivity that economists measure. Labour productivity can be measured for a firm, a process or a country.

Consumption function

In economics, the Consumption function is a single mathematical function used to express consumer spending. It was developed by John Maynard Keynes and detailed most famously in his book The General Theory of Employment, Interest, and Money. The function is used to calculate the amount of total consumption in an economy.

Disposable income

Disposable income is total personal income minus personal current taxes. In national accounts definitions, personal income, minus personal current taxes equals disposable personal income. Subtracting personal outlays yields personal savings.

Interest rate

An Interest rate is the price a borrower pays for the use of money they borrow from a lender, for instance a small company might borrow capital from a bank to buy new assets for their business, and the return a lender receives for deferring the use of funds, by lending it to the borrower. Interests rates are fundamental to a capitalist society. Interest rates are normally expressed as a percentage rate over the period of one year.

Investment function

The Investment function is a summary of the variables that influence the levels of aggregate investments. It can be formalized as follows:

I=I(r,ΔY,q)

- + +

where r is the real interest rate, Y the GDP and q is Tobin`s q. The signs under the variables simply tell us if the variable influences investment in a positive or negative way (for instance, if real interest rates were to rise, investments would correspondingly fall).

Nominal interest rate	In finance and economics Nominal interest rate refers to the rate of interest before adjustment for inflation (in contrast with the real interest rate); or, for interest rates `as stated` without adjustment for the full effect of compounding (also referred to as the nominal annual rate). An interest rate is called nominal if the frequency of compounding (e.g. a month) is not identical to the basic time unit (normally a year).
Real interest rate	The Real interest rate is approximately the nominal interest rate minus the inflation rate. It is the rate of interest an investor expects to receive after subtracting inflation. This is not a single number, as different investors have different expectations of future inflation. If, for example, an investor were able to lock in a 5% interest rate for the coming year and anticipated a 2% rise in prices, it would expect to earn a Real interest rate of 3%.
Bond	In finance, a bond is a debt security, in which the authorized issuer owes the holders a debt and, depending on the terms of the bond, is obliged to pay interest (the coupon) and/or to repay the principal at a later date, termed maturity. A bond is a formal contract to repay borrowed money with interest at fixed intervals. Thus a bond is like a loan: the issuer is the borrower (debtor), the holder is the lender (creditor), and the coupon is the interest.
Credit risk	Credit risk is an investor`s risk of loss arising from a borrower who does not make payments as promised. Such an event is called a default. Another term for Credit risk is default risk. Investor losses include lost principal and interest, decreased cash flow, and increased collection costs, which arise in a number of circumstances: · A consumer does not make a payment due on a mortgage loan, credit card, line of credit, or other loan · A business does not make a payment due on a mortgage, credit card, line of credit, or other loan · A business or consumer does not pay a trade invoice when due · A business does not pay an employee`s earned wages when due

· A business or government bond issuer does not make a payment on a coupon or principal payment when due

· An insolvent insurance company does not pay a policy obligation

· An insolvent bank won`t return funds to a depositor

· A government grants bankruptcy protection to an insolvent consumer or business

Significant resources and sophisticated programs are used to analyze and manage risk.

Municipal bond

A Municipal bond is a bond issued by a city or other local government, or their agencies. Potential issuers of Municipal bonds include cities, counties, redevelopment agencies, special-purpose districts, school districts, public utility districts, publicly owned airports and seaports, and any other governmental entity (or group of governments) below the state level. Municipal bonds may be general obligations of the issuer or secured by specified revenues.

Balanced budget

A Balanced budget is when there is neither a budget deficit or a budget surplus - when revenues equal expenditure (`the accounts balance`) - particularly by a government. More generally, it refers to when there is no deficit, but possibly a surplus. A cyclically Balanced budget is a budget that is not necessarily balanced year-to-year, but is balanced over the economic cycle, running a surplus in boom years and running a deficit in lean years, with these offsetting over time.

Keynesian cross

In the Keynesian cross diagram is a desired total spending (or aggregate expenditure, or `aggregate demand`) curve (shown in blue) is drawn as a rising line since consumers will have a larger demand with a rise in disposable income, which increases with total national output. This increase is due to the positive relationship between consumption and consumers` disposable income in the consumption function. Aggregate demand may also rise due to increases in investment (due to the accelerator effect), while this rise is reduced if imports and tax revenues rise with income. Equilibrium in this diagram occurs where total demand, AD, equals the total amount of national output, Y. Here, total demand equals total supply.

Long-run

In economic models, the Long-run time frame assumes no fixed factors of production. Firms can enter or leave the marketplace, and the cost (and availability) of land, labor, capital goods and entrepreneurship can be assumed to vary. In contrast, in the short-run time frame, certain factors are assumed to be fixed.

Financial market

In economics, a Financial market is a mechanism that allows people to buy and sell (trade) financial securities (such as stocks and bonds), commodities , and other fungible items of value at low transaction costs and at prices that reflect the efficient-market hypothesis.

Both general markets (where many commodities are traded) and specialized markets (where only one commodity is traded) exist. Markets work by placing many interested buyers and sellers in one `place`, thus making it easier for them to find each other.

Loanable funds

In economics, the Loanable funds market is a hypothetical market that brings savers and borrowers together, also bringing together the money available in commercial banks and lending institutions available for firms and households to finance expenditures, either investments or consumption. Savers supply the Loanable funds; for instance, buying bonds will transfer their money to the institution issuing the bond, which can be a firm or government. In return, borrowers demand Loanable funds; when an institution sells a bond, it is demanding Loanable funds.

Fiscal policy

In economics, Fiscal policy is the use of government expenditure and revenue collection to influence the economy.

Fiscal policy can be contrasted with the other main type of macroeconomic policy, monetary policy, which attempts to stabilize the economy by controlling interest rates and the supply of money. The two main instruments of Fiscal policy are government expenditure and taxation. Changes in the level and composition of taxation and government spending can impact on the following variables in the economy:

· Aggregate demand and the level of economic activity;

· The pattern of resource allocation;

· The distribution of income

Fiscal policy refers to the use of the government budget to influence the first of these: economic activity.

Crowding out

In economics,`Crowding out` is any reduction in private consumption or investment that occurs because of an increase in government spending. If the increase in government spending is financed by a tax increase, the tax increase would tend to reduce private consumption. If instead the increase in government spending is not accompanied by a tax increase, government borrowing to finance the increased government spending would increase interest rates, leading to a reduction in private investment.

Financial system

In finance, the Financial system is the system that allows the transfer of money between savers and borrowers. It comprises a set of complex and closely interconnected financial institutions, markets, instruments, services, practices, and transactions.

Financial systems are crucial to the allocation of resources in a modern economy.

Recession

In economics, a Recession is a business cycle contraction, a general slowdown in economic activity over a period of time. During Recessions, many macroeconomic indicators vary in a similar way. Production as measured by Gross Domestic Product (GDP), employment, investment spending, capacity utilization, household incomes, business profits and inflation all fall during Recessions; while bankruptcies and the unemployment rate rise.

Stock

The Stock or capital Stock of a business entity represents the original capital paid into or invested in the business by its founders. It serves as a security for the creditors of a business since it cannot be withdrawn to the detriment of the creditors. Stock is distinct from the property and the assets of a business which may fluctuate in quantity and value.

Financial crisis

The term Financial crisis is applied broadly to a variety of situations in which some financial institutions or assets suddenly lose a large part of their value. In the 19th and early 20th centuries, many financial crises were associated with banking panics, and many recessions coincided with these panics. Other situations that are often called financial crises include stock market crashes and the bursting of other financial bubbles, currency crises, and sovereign defaults.

Short-run

In economics, the concept of the Short-run refers to the decision-making time frame of a firm in which at least one factor of production is fixed. Costs which are fixed in the Short-run have no impact on a firm decisions. For example a firm can raise output by increasing the amount of labor through overtime.

A generic firm can make three changes in the Short-run:

· Increase production

· Decrease production

· Shut down

In the Short-run, a profit maximizing firm will:

· Increase production if marginal cost is less than price;

· Decrease production if marginal cost is greater than price;

· Continue producing if average variable cost is less than price, even if average total cost is greater than price;

· Shut down if average variable cost is greater than price.

Government bond

A bond is a debt investment in which an investor loans a certain amount of money, for a certain amount of time, with a certain interest rate, to a company. A Government bond is a bond issued by a national government denominated in the country`s own currency. Bonds issued by national governments in foreign currencies are normally referred to as sovereign bonds.

Collective bargaining

Collective bargaining is a process between employers and employees to reach an agreement regarding the rights and duties of people at work. Collective bargaining aims to reach a collective agreement which usually sets out issues such as employees pay, working hours, training, health and safety, and rights to participate in workplace or company affairs.

During the bargaining process, employees are typically represented by a trade union.

Devaluation

Devaluation comes from the word `devalue`, which according to Merriam-Webster means `to lessen the value of.` As such, `Devaluation` is a reduction in the value of a currency with respect to those goods, services or other monetary units with which that currency can be exchanged.

In common modern usage, it specifically implies an official lowering of the value of a country`s currency within a fixed exchange rate system, by which the monetary authority formally sets a new fixed rate with respect to a foreign reference currency. In contrast, depreciation is used for the unofficial decrease in the exchange rate in a floating exchange rate system.

Aggregate Demand-Aggregate Supply model	Aggregate Demand-Aggregate Supply model is a macroeconomic model that explains price level and output through the relationship of aggregate demand and aggregate supply. It was first put forth by John Maynard Keynes in his work The General Theory of Employment, Interest, and Money. It is the foundation for the modern field of macroeconomics, and is accepted by a broad array of economists, from Libertarian, Monetarist supporters of laissez-faire, such as Milton Friedman to Socialist, Post-Keynesian supporters of economic interventionism, such as Joan Robinson.
Deflation	Deflation is a decrease in the general price level of goods and services. Deflation occurs when the annual inflation rate falls below zero percent (a negative inflation rate), resulting in an increase in the real value of money - allowing one to buy more goods with the same amount of money. This should not be confused with disinflation, a slow-down in the inflation rate.
Real gross domestic product	Real gross domestic product is a macroeconomic measure of the size of an economy adjusted for price changes Gross domestic product is defined as the market value of all final goods and services produced in a geographical region, usually a country. That market value depends on two things: the actual quantity of goods and services produced, and their price. The actual quantity of goods and services produced is sometimes called the volume.
Hyperinflation	Hyperinflation is inflation that is very high or `out of control`, a condition in which prices increase rapidly as a currency loses its value. Definitions used by the media vary from a cumulative inflation rate over three years approaching 100% to `inflation exceeding 50% a month.` In informal usage the term is often applied to much lower rates. As a rule of thumb, normal inflation is reported per year, but Hyperinflation is often reported for much shorter intervals, often per month.
Inflation	In economics, Inflation is a rise in the general level of prices of goods and services in an economy over a period of time. When the price level rises, each unit of currency buys fewer goods and services; consequently, annual Inflation is also an erosion in the purchasing power of money - a loss of real value in the internal medium of exchange and unit of account in the economy. A chief measure of price Inflation is the Inflation rate, the annualized percentage change in a general price index over time.
Collective bargaining	Collective bargaining is a process between employers and employees to reach an agreement regarding the rights and duties of people at work. Collective bargaining aims to reach a collective agreement which usually sets out issues such as employees pay, working hours, training, health and safety, and rights to participate in workplace or company affairs. During the bargaining process, employees are typically represented by a trade union.

Economic growth	Economic growth is a term used to indicate the increase of per capita gross domestic product (GDP) or other measure of aggregate income. It is often measured as the rate of change in GDP. Economic growth refers only to the quantity of goods and services produced.
Government debt	Government debt is money (or credit) owed by any level of government; either central government, federal government, municipal government or local government. By contrast, annual government deficit refers to the difference between government receipts and spending in a single year. Debt of a sovereign government is called sovereign debt.
Interest rate	An Interest rate is the price a borrower pays for the use of money they borrow from a lender, for instance a small company might borrow capital from a bank to buy new assets for their business, and the return a lender receives for deferring the use of funds, by lending it to the borrower. Interests rates are fundamental to a capitalist society. Interest rates are normally expressed as a percentage rate over the period of one year.
Money	Money is anything that is generally accepted as payment for goods and services and repayment of debts. The main functions of Money are distinguished as: a medium of exchange; a unit of account; a store of value; and, occasionally, a standard of deferred payment. Money originated as commodity Money, but nearly all contemporary Money systems are based on fiat Money.
Nominal interest rate	In finance and economics Nominal interest rate refers to the rate of interest before adjustment for inflation (in contrast with the real interest rate); or, for interest rates `as stated` without adjustment for the full effect of compounding (also referred to as the nominal annual rate). An interest rate is called nominal if the frequency of compounding (e.g. a month) is not identical to the basic time unit (normally a year).
Inflation tax	An Inflation tax is the economic disadvantage suffered by holders of cash and cash equivalents in one denomination of currency due to the effects of Expansionary monetary policy, which acts as a hidden tax that subtracts value from those assets. Many economists hold that the Inflation tax affects the lower and middle classes more than the rich, as they hold a larger fraction of their income in cash, they are much less likely to receive the newly created monies before the market has adjusted with inflated prices, and more often have fixed incomes, wages or pensions. Some argue that inflation is a regressive consumption tax.

Store of value	A recognized form of exchange can be a form of money or currency, a commodity like gold, or financial capital. To act as a Store of value, these forms must be able to be saved and retrieved at a later time, and be predictably useful when retrieved. Storage of value is one of several distinct functions of money. The other functions are the standard of deferred payment, which requires acceptability to parties owed a debt, and the unit of account, which requires fungibility so accounts in any amount can be readily settled. It is also distinct from the medium of exchange function which requires durability when used in trade and to minimize fraud opportunities.
Unit of account	A Unit of account is a standard monetary unit of measurement of the market value/cost of goods, services, or assets. It is one of three well-known functions of money. It lends meaning to profits, losses, liability, or assets.
Commodity	A Commodity is a good for which there is demand, but which is supplied without qualitative differentiation across a market. It is fungible, i.e. the same no matter who produces it. Examples are petroleum, notebook paper, milk or copper.
Commodity money	Commodity money is money whose value comes from a commodity out of which it is made. It is objects that have value in themselves as well as for use as money.
Exchange	An exchange is a highly organized market where (especially) tradable securities, commodities, foreign exchange, futures, and options contracts are sold and bought. exchanges bring together brokers and dealers who buy and sell these objects. These various financial instruments can typically be sold either through the exchange, typically with the benefit of a clearinghouse to cover defaults, or over-the-counter, where there is typically less protection against counterparty risk from clearinghouses although OTC clearinghouses have become more common over the years, with regulators placing pressure on the OTC markets to clear and display trades openly.
Fiat money	The term Fiat money is used to mean: · any money declared by a government to be legal tender. · state-issued money which is neither legally convertible to any other thing, nor fixed in value in terms of any objective standard.

· money without intrinsic value.

The term derives from the Latin fiat, meaning `let it be done`, as the money is established by government decree. Where Fiat money is used as currency, the term fiat currency is used.

Gold standard

The Gold standard is a monetary system in which the standard economic unit of account is a fixed weight of gold. Three distinct kinds of Gold standard can be identified. The gold specie standard is a system in which the monetary unit is associated with circulating gold coins, or with the unit of value defined in terms of one particular circulating gold coin in conjunction with subsidiary coinage made from a lesser valuable metal.

Medium of exchange

A Medium of exchange is an intermediary used in trade to avoid the inconveniences of a pure barter system.

By contrast, as William Stanley Jevons argued, in a barter system there must be a coincidence of wants before two people can trade - one must want exactly what the other has to offer, when and where it is offered, so that the exchange can occur. A Medium of exchange permits the value of goods to be assessed and rendered in terms of the intermediary, most often, a form of money widely accepted to buy any other good.

Coincidence of wants

The Coincidence of wants problem is an important category of transaction costs that impose severe limitations on economies lacking money and thus dominated by barter or other in-kind transactions. The problem is caused by the improbability of the wants, needs or events that cause or motivate a transaction occurring at the same time and the same place. One example is the bar musician who is `paid` with liquor or food, items which his landlord will not accept as rent payment, when the musician would rather have a month`s shelter.

Demand

In economics, demand is the desire to own anything and the ability to pay for it and willingness to pay . The term demand signifies the ability or the willingness to buy a particular commodity at a given point of time.

Economists record demand on a demand schedule and plot it on a graph as a demand curve that is usually downward sloping.

Demand for Money	The Demand for money is the desired holding of money balances in the form of cash or bank deposits. Money is dominated as store of value by interest-bearing assets. However, money is necessary to carry out transactions, or in other words, it provides liquidity.
Exchange rate	In finance, the Exchange rates between two currencies specifies how much one currency is worth in terms of the other. It is the value of a foreign nation`s currency in terms of the home nation`s currency.
Mundell-Fleming model	The Mundell-Fleming model is an economic model first set forth by Robert Mundell and Marcus Fleming. The model is an extension of the IS-LM model. Whereas the traditional IS-LM Model deals with economy under autarky (or a closed economy), the Mundell-Fleming model tries to describe an open economy.
Capital	In economics, capital, capital goods, or real capital are factors of production used to create goods or services that are not themselves significantly consumed (though they may depreciate) in the production process. capital goods may be acquired with money or financial capital. In finance and accounting, capital generally refers to saved-up financial wealth, especially that used to start or maintain a business.
Good	In economics and accounting, a good is physical product that can be used to satisfy some desire or need. It can be contrasted with a service which is intangible, whereas a good is a tangible physical product, capable of being delivered to a purchaser and involves the transfer of ownership from seller to customer. For example, an apple is a tangible good, as opposed to a haircut, which is an (intangible) service.
Inflation rate	In economics, the Inflation rate is a measure of inflation, the rate of increase of a price index . It is the percentage rate of change in price level over time. The rate of decrease in the purchasing power of money is approximately equal. The Inflation rate is used to calculate the real interest rate, as well as real increases in wages, and official measurements of this rate act as input variables to COLA adjustments and inflation derivatives prices.
Monetary policy	Monetary policy is the process by which the central bank or monetary authority of a country controls the supply of money and the rate of interest. Monetary policy is usually used to attain a set of objectives oriented towards the growth and stability of the economy. These goals usually include stable prices and low unemployment.

Chapter 4. Money and Inflation

Money supply	In economics, Money supply is the total amount of money available in an economy at a particular point in time. There are several ways to define \`money,\` but standard measures usually include currency in circulation and demand deposits. Money supply data are recorded and published, usually by the government or the central bank of the country. Public and private-sector analysts have long monitored changes in Money supply because of its possible effects on the price level, inflation and the business cycle.
Central bank	A Central bank, reserve bank, or monetary authority is a banking institution granted the exclusive privilege to lend a government its currency. Like a normal commercial bank, a Central bank charges interest on the loans made to borrowers, primarily the government of whichever country the bank exists for, and to other commercial banks, typically as a \`lender of last resort\`. However, a Central bank is distinguished from a normal commercial bank because it has a monopoly on creating the currency of that nation, which is loaned to the government in the form of legal tender.
Federal Reserve System	The Federal Reserve System is the central banking system of the United States. It was created in 1913 with the enactment of the Federal Reserve Act, and was largely a response to a series of financial panics, particularly a severe panic in 1907. Over time, the roles and responsibilities of the Federal Reserve System have expanded and its structure has evolved.
Investment	Investment is the commitment of money or capital to purchase financial instruments or other assets in order to gain profitable returns in form of interest, income, or appreciation of the value of the instrument. It is related to saving or deferring consumption. Investment is involved in many areas of the economy, such as business management and finance no matter for households, firms, or governments.
Quantity theory of money	In monetary economics, the Quantity theory of money is the theory that money supply has a direct, positive relationship with the price level. The theory was challenged by Keynesian economics, but updated and reinvigorated by the monetarist school of economics. While mainstream economists agree that the quantity theory holds true in the long-run, there is still disagreement about its applicability in the short-run.
Velocity of money	The Velocity of money is the average frequency with which a unit of money is spent in a specific period of time. Velocity associates the amount of economic activity associated with a given money supply. When the period is understood, the velocity may be present as a pure number; otherwise it should be given as a pure number over time.

Income	Income is the consumption and savings opportunity gained by an entity within a specified time frame, which is generally expressed in monetary terms. However, for households and individuals, `Income is the sum of all the wages, salaries, profits, interests payments, rents and other forms of earnings received... in a given period of time.` For firms, Income generally refers to net-profit: what remains of revenue after expenses have been subtracted.
Factors of production	In economics, Factors of production are the resources employed to produce goods and services. They facilitate production but do not become part of the product (as with raw materials) or become significantly transformed by the production process . To 19th century economists, the Factors of production were land (natural resources, gifts from nature), labor (the ability to work), capital goods (human-made tools and equipment) and enterprise.
Price level	A Price level is a hypothetical measure of overall prices for some set of goods and services, in a given region during a given interval, normalized relative to some base set. Typically, a Price level is approximated with a price index.
Seigniorage	Seigniorage can have the following two meanings: · Seigniorage derived from specie--metal coins, is a tax, added to the total price of a coin , that a customer of the mint had to pay to the mint, and that was sent to the sovereign of the political area. · Seigniorage derived from notes is more indirect, being the difference between interest earned on securities acquired in exchange for bank notes and the costs of producing and distributing those notes. Seigniorage is a convenient source of revenue for some national banks. In macroeconomics, Seigniorage is regarded as a form of inflation tax, as paying for government services by issuing new currency has the effect of creating a de facto tax that falls on those who hold the existing currency, as a result of its effective devaluation through the introduction of additional money.

Chapter 4. Money and Inflation

Fisher equation	The Fisher equation in financial mathematics and economics estimates the relationship between nominal and real interest rates under inflation. It is named after Irving Fisher who was famous for his works on the theory of interest. In finance, the Fisher equation is primarily used in YTM calculations of bonds or IRR calculations of investments. In economics, this equation is used to predict nominal and real interest rate behavior.
Coinage Act	The Coinage Act or the Mint Act, passed by the United States Congress on April 2, 1792, established the United States Mint and regulated the coinage of the United States. The long title of the legislation is An act establishing a mint, and regulating the Coins of the United States. This act established the dollar as the unit of money in the United States, declared it to be lawful tender, and created a decimal system for U.S. currency.
Real interest rate	The Real interest rate is approximately the nominal interest rate minus the inflation rate. It is the rate of interest an investor expects to receive after subtracting inflation. This is not a single number, as different investors have different expectations of future inflation. If, for example, an investor were able to lock in a 5% interest rate for the coming year and anticipated a 2% rise in prices, it would expect to earn a Real interest rate of 3%.
Keynesian cross	In the Keynesian cross diagram is a desired total spending (or aggregate expenditure, or `aggregate demand`) curve (shown in blue) is drawn as a rising line since consumers will have a larger demand with a rise in disposable income, which increases with total national output. This increase is due to the positive relationship between consumption and consumers` disposable income in the consumption function. Aggregate demand may also rise due to increases in investment (due to the accelerator effect), while this rise is reduced if imports and tax revenues rise with income. Equilibrium in this diagram occurs where total demand, AD, equals the total amount of national output, Y. Here, total demand equals total supply.
Circular flow of income	In neoclassical economics, the terms Circular flow of income refer to a simple economic model which describes the reciprocal circulation of income between producers and consumers. In the circular flow model, the inter-dependent entities of producer and consumer are referred to as `firms` and `households` respectively and provide each other with factors in order to facilitate the flow of income. Firms provide consumers with goods and services in exchange for consumer expenditure and `factors of production` from households.
Consumer price index	A Consumer price index is a measure estimating the average price of consumer goods and services purchased by households. A Consumer price index measures a price change for a constant market basket of goods and services from one period to the next within the same area (city, region, or nation). It is a price index determined by measuring the price of a standard group of goods meant to represent the typical market basket of a typical urban consumer.

Cost	In business, retail, and accounting, a Cost is the value of money that has been used up to produce something, and hence is not available for use anymore. In economics, a Cost is an alternative that is given up as a result of a decision. In business, the Cost may be one of acquisition, in which case the amount of money expended to acquire it is counted as Cost.
Cost of capital	The Cost of capital is the cost of a company`s funds (both debt and equity), or, from an investor`s point of view `the expected return on a portfolio of all the company`s existing securities`. It is used to evaluate new projects of a company as it is the minimum return that investors expect for providing capital to the company, thus setting a benchmark that a new project has to meet. For an investment to be worthwhile, the expected return on capital must be greater than the Cost of capital.
Social cost	Social cost, in economics, is generally defined in opposition to `private cost`. In economics, theorists model individual decision-making as measurement of costs and benefits. Rational choice theory often assumes that individuals consider only the costs they themselves bear when making decisions, not the costs that may be borne by others.
Menu costs	In economics, Menu costs are the costs to firms of updating menus, price lists, brochures, and other materials when prices change in an economy. Because this transaction cost exists, firms sometimes do not change their prices when the economy puts pressure on it, leading to price stickiness. Generally, the effect on the firm of small shifts in price are relatively minor compared to the costs of notifying the public of this new information.
Bretton Woods system	The Bretton Woods system is commonly understood to refer to the international monetary regime that prevailed from the end of World War II until the early 1970s. Taking its name from the site of the 1944 conference that created the International Monetary Fund (IMF) and World Bank, the Bretton Woods system was history`s first example of a fully negotiated monetary order intended to govern currency relations among sovereign states. In principle, the regime was designed to combine binding legal obligations with multilateral decision-making conducted through an international organization, the IMF, endowed with limited supranational authority.
Indexation	Indexation is a technique to adjust income payments by means of a price index, in order to maintain the purchasing power of the public after inflation.

Applying a cost-of-living escalation COLA clause to a stream of periodic payments protects the real value of those payments and effectively transfers the risk of inflation from the payee to the payor, who must pay more each year to reflect the increases in prices. Thus, inflation Indexation is often applied to pension payments, rents and other situations which are not subje market.

Risk aversion

Risk aversion is a concept in psychology, economics, and finance, based on the behavior of humans (especially consumers and investors) whilst exposed to uncertainty.

Risk aversion is the reluctance of a person to accept a bargain with an uncertain payoff rather than another bargain with a more certain, but possibly lower, expected payoff. For example, a risk-averse investor might choose to put his or her money into a bank account with a low but guaranteed interest rate, rather than into a stock that may have high returns, but also has a chance of becoming worthless.

Real wages

The term Real wages refers to wages that have been adjusted for inflation. This term is used in contrast to nominal wages or unadjusted wages.

The use of adjusted figures is used in undertaking some forms of economic analysis.

Hyperinflation in Zimbabwe

Hyperinflation in Zimbabwe began in the early 2000s, shortly after Zimbabwe`s confiscation of white-owned farmland and its repudiation of debts to the International Monetary Fund, and persisted through to 2009. Figures from November 2008 estimated Zimbabwe`s annual inflation rate at 89.7 sextillion (10^{21}) percent. By December 2008, inflation was estimated at quindecillion novemdecillion percent (6.5×10^{108}%, or 65 followed by 107 zeros). In April 2009, Zimbabwe abandoned printing of the Zimbabwean dollar, and the South African rand and US dollar became the standard currencies for exchange. The government does not intend to reintroduce the currency until 2010.

Marginal propensity to consume

In economics, the Marginal propensity to consume is an empirical metric that quantifies induced consumption, the concept that the increase in personal consumer spending (consumption) that occurs with an increase in disposable income (income after taxes and transfers). For example, if a household earns one extra dollar of disposable income, and the Marginal propensity to consume is 0.65, then of that dollar, the household will spend 65 cents and save 35 cents.

Mathematically, the Marginal propensity to consume function is expressed as the derivative of the consumption (C) function with respect to disposable income (Y).

$$MPC = \frac{dC}{dY}$$

OR

$$MPC = \frac{\Delta C}{\Delta Y}$$

, where ΔC is the change in consumption, and ΔY is the change in disposable income that produced the consumption.

Classical dichotomy

In macroeconomics, the Classical dichotomy refers to an idea attributed to classical and pre-Keynesian economics that real and nominal variables can be analyzed separately. To be precise, an economy exhibits the Classical dichotomy if real variables such as output and real interest rates can be completely analyzed without considering what is happening to their nominal counterparts, the money value of output and the interest rate. In particular, this means that real GDP and other real variables can be determined without knowing the level of the nominal money supply or the rate of inflation.

Chapter 5. The Open Economy

Capital	In economics, capital, capital goods, or real capital are factors of production used to create goods or services that are not themselves significantly consumed (though they may depreciate) in the production process. capital goods may be acquired with money or financial capital. In finance and accounting, capital generally refers to saved-up financial wealth, especially that used to start or maintain a business.
Good	In economics and accounting, a good is physical product that can be used to satisfy some desire or need. It can be contrasted with a service which is intangible, whereas a good is a tangible physical product, capable of being delivered to a purchaser and involves the transfer of ownership from seller to customer. For example, an apple is a tangible good, as opposed to a haircut, which is an (intangible) service.
Balance of trade	The Balance of trade is the difference between the monetary value of exports and imports of output in an economy over a certain period. It is the relationship between a nation`s imports and exports. A positive or favorable Balance of trade is known as a trade surplus if it consists of exporting more than is imported; a negative or unfavorable balance is referred to as a trade deficit or, informally, a trade gap. The Balance of trade is sometimes divided into a goods and a services balance.
Net capital outflow	Net Capital Outflow is the net flow of funds being invested abroad by a country during a certain period of time (usually a year). A positive Net Capital Outflow means that the country invests outside more than the world invests in it; a negative one, that the world invests in the country more than the country invests in the world. Net Capital Outflow is one of two major ways of characterizing the nature of a country`s financial and economic interaction with the rest of the world (the other being the balance of trade).
Investment	Investment is the commitment of money or capital to purchase financial instruments or other assets in order to gain profitable returns in form of interest, income, or appreciation of the value of the instrument. It is related to saving or deferring consumption. Investment is involved in many areas of the economy, such as business management and finance no matter for households, firms, or governments.
Balanced trade	Balanced trade is an alternative economic model to free trade. Under Balanced trade nations are required to provide a fairly even reciprocal trade pattern; they cannot run large trade deficits.

The concept of Balanced trade arises from an essay by Michael McKeever Sr. of the McKeever Institute of Economic Policy Analysis. According to the essay, `Balanced trade is a simple concept which says that a country should import only as much as it exports so that trade and money flows are balanced. A country can balance its trade either on a trading partner basis in which total money flows between two countries are equalized or it can balance the overall trade and money flows so that a trade deficit with one country is balanced by a trade surplus with another country.`

Surplus

The term surplus is used in economics for several related quantities. The consumer surplus is the amount that consumers benefit by being able to purchase a product for a price that is less than the most that they would be willing to pay. The producer surplus is the amount that producers benefit by selling at a market price mechanism that is higher than the least that they would be willing to sell for.

Government debt

Government debt is money (or credit) owed by any level of government; either central government, federal government, municipal government or local government. By contrast, annual government deficit refers to the difference between government receipts and spending in a single year. Debt of a sovereign government is called sovereign debt.

Interest rate

An Interest rate is the price a borrower pays for the use of money they borrow from a lender, for instance a small company might borrow capital from a bank to buy new assets for their business, and the return a lender receives for deferring the use of funds, by lending it to the borrower. Interests rates are fundamental to a capitalist society. Interest rates are normally expressed as a percentage rate over the period of one year.

Mundell-Fleming model

The Mundell-Fleming model is an economic model first set forth by Robert Mundell and Marcus Fleming. The model is an extension of the IS-LM model. Whereas the traditional IS-LM Model deals with economy under autarky (or a closed economy), the Mundell-Fleming model tries to describe an open economy.

Fiscal policy

In economics, Fiscal policy is the use of government expenditure and revenue collection to influence the economy.

Fiscal policy can be contrasted with the other main type of macroeconomic policy, monetary policy, which attempts to stabilize the economy by controlling interest rates and the supply of money. The two main instruments of Fiscal policy are government expenditure and taxation. Changes in the level and composition of taxation and government spending can impact on the following variables in the economy:

· Aggregate demand and the level of economic activity;

· The pattern of resource allocation;

· The distribution of income

Fiscal policy refers to the use of the government budget to influence the first of these: economic activity.

Demand

In economics, demand is the desire to own anything and the ability to pay for it and willingness to pay . The term demand signifies the ability or the willingness to buy a particular commodity at a given point of time.

Economists record demand on a demand schedule and plot it on a graph as a demand curve that is usually downward sloping.

Economic growth

Economic growth is a term used to indicate the increase of per capita gross domestic product (GDP) or other measure of aggregate income. It is often measured as the rate of change in GDP. Economic growth refers only to the quantity of goods and services produced.

Income

Income is the consumption and savings opportunity gained by an entity within a specified time frame, which is generally expressed in monetary terms. However, for households and individuals, `Income is the sum of all the wages, salaries, profits, interests payments, rents and other forms of earnings received... in a given period of time.` For firms, Income generally refers to net-profit: what remains of revenue after expenses have been subtracted.

Inflation

In economics, Inflation is a rise in the general level of prices of goods and services in an economy over a period of time. When the price level rises, each unit of currency buys fewer goods and services; consequently, annual Inflation is also an erosion in the purchasing power of money - a loss of real value in the internal medium of exchange and unit of account in the economy. A chief measure of price Inflation is the Inflation rate, the annualized percentage change in a general price index over time.

Population growth

In demography, Population growth is used informally for the more specific term Population growth rate , and is often used to refer specifically to the growth of the human population of the world.

Simple models of Population growth include the Malthusian Growth Model and the logistic model.

In demographics and ecology, Population growth rate (PGR) is the fractional rate at which the number of individuals in a population increases.

Stagflation

In economics, the term Stagflation refers to the situation when both the inflation rate and the unemployment rate are high. It is a difficult economic condition for a country, as both inflation and economic stagnation occur simultaneously and no macroeconomic policy can address both of these problems at the same time.

The portmanteau Stagflation is generally attributed to British politician Iain Macleod, who coined the term in a speech to Parliament in 1965.

Tax cut

Economic stimulus via Tax cuts, along with interest rate intervention and deficit spending, are one of the central tenets of Keynesian economics.

The immediate effects of a Tax cut are, generally, a decrease in the real income of the government and an increase in the real income of those whose tax rate has been lowered.

Export-oriented industrialization

Export-oriented industrialization is a trade and economic policy aiming to speed-up the industrialization process of a country through exporting goods for which the nation has a comparative advantage. Export-led growth implies opening domestic markets to foreign competition in exchange for market access in other countries, though this may not be true of all domestic markets as governments aim to protect specific nascent industries so they grow and are able to exploit their future comparative advantage and in practise the converse can occur, for example many East Asian countries had strong barriers on imports during most of the 1960s-1980s. Reduced tariff barriers, floating exchange rate (devaluation of national currency is often employed to facilitate exports), and government support for exporting sectors are all an example of policies adopted to promote Export oriented industrialization, and ultimately economic development.

Cost

In business, retail, and accounting, a Cost is the value of money that has been used up to produce something, and hence is not available for use anymore. In economics, a Cost is an alternative that is given up as a result of a decision. In business, the Cost may be one of acquisition, in which case the amount of money expended to acquire it is counted as Cost.

Chapter 5. The Open Economy

Economic policy	Economic policy refers to the actions that governments take in the economic field. It covers the systems for setting interest rates and government budget as well as the labour market, national ownership, and many other areas of government interventions into the economy. Such policies are often influenced by international institutions like the International Monetary Fund or World Bank as well as political beliefs and the consequent policies of parties.
Exchange	An exchange is a highly organized market where (especially) tradable securities, commodities, foreign exchange, futures, and options contracts are sold and bought. exchanges bring together brokers and dealers who buy and sell these objects. These various financial instruments can typically be sold either through the exchange, typically with the benefit of a clearinghouse to cover defaults, or over-the-counter, where there is typically less protection against counterparty risk from clearinghouses although OTC clearinghouses have become more common over the years, with regulators placing pressure on the OTC markets to clear and display trades openly.
Exchange rate	In finance, the Exchange rates between two currencies specifies how much one currency is worth in terms of the other. It is the value of a foreign nation`s currency in terms of the home nation`s currency.
Appreciation	In accounting, Appreciation of an asset is an increase in its value. In this sense it is the reverse of depreciation, which measures the fall in value of assets over their normal life-time. Generally, the term is reserved for property or, more specifically, land and buildings.
Depreciation	Depreciation is a term used in accounting, economics and finance to spread the cost of an asset over the span of several years. In accounting, however, Depreciation is a term used to describe any method of attributing the historical or purchase cost of an asset across its useful life, roughly corresponding to normal wear and tear.
Determinant	In algebra, the Determinant is a special number associated with any square matrix. The fundamental geometric meaning of a Determinant is a scale factor for measure when the matrix is regarded as a linear transformation. Thus a 2 × 2 matrix with Determinant 2 when applied to a set of points with finite area will transform those points into a set with twice the area.

Aggregate Demand-Aggregate Supply model	Aggregate Demand-Aggregate Supply model is a macroeconomic model that explains price level and output through the relationship of aggregate demand and aggregate supply. It was first put forth by John Maynard Keynes in his work The General Theory of Employment, Interest, and Money. It is the foundation for the modern field of macroeconomics, and is accepted by a broad array of economists, from Libertarian, Monetarist supporters of laissez-faire, such as Milton Friedman to Socialist, Post-Keynesian supporters of economic interventionism, such as Joan Robinson.
Deflation	Deflation is a decrease in the general price level of goods and services. Deflation occurs when the annual inflation rate falls below zero percent (a negative inflation rate), resulting in an increase in the real value of money - allowing one to buy more goods with the same amount of money. This should not be confused with disinflation, a slow-down in the inflation rate.
Real gross domestic product	Real gross domestic product is a macroeconomic measure of the size of an economy adjusted for price changes Gross domestic product is defined as the market value of all final goods and services produced in a geographical region, usually a country. That market value depends on two things: the actual quantity of goods and services produced, and their price. The actual quantity of goods and services produced is sometimes called the volume.
Hyperinflation	Hyperinflation is inflation that is very high or \`out of control\`, a condition in which prices increase rapidly as a currency loses its value. Definitions used by the media vary from a cumulative inflation rate over three years approaching 100% to \`inflation exceeding 50% a month.\` In informal usage the term is often applied to much lower rates. As a rule of thumb, normal inflation is reported per year, but Hyperinflation is often reported for much shorter intervals, often per month.
Collective bargaining	Collective bargaining is a process between employers and employees to reach an agreement regarding the rights and duties of people at work. Collective bargaining aims to reach a collective agreement which usually sets out issues such as employees pay, working hours, training, health and safety, and rights to participate in workplace or company affairs. During the bargaining process, employees are typically represented by a trade union.
Money	Money is anything that is generally accepted as payment for goods and services and repayment of debts. The main functions of Money are distinguished as: a medium of exchange; a unit of account; a store of value; and, occasionally, a standard of deferred payment.

	Money originated as commodity Money, but nearly all contemporary Money systems are based on fiat Money.
Nominal interest rate	In finance and economics Nominal interest rate refers to the rate of interest before adjustment for inflation (in contrast with the real interest rate); or, for interest rates `as stated` without adjustment for the full effect of compounding (also referred to as the nominal annual rate). An interest rate is called nominal if the frequency of compounding (e.g. a month) is not identical to the basic time unit (normally a year).
Consumer price index	A Consumer price index is a measure estimating the average price of consumer goods and services purchased by households. A Consumer price index measures a price change for a constant market basket of goods and services from one period to the next within the same area (city, region, or nation). It is a price index determined by measuring the price of a standard group of goods meant to represent the typical market basket of a typical urban consumer.
Law of one price	The Law of one price is an economic law stated as: `In an efficient market all identical goods must have only one price.` The intuition for this law is that all sellers will flock to the highest prevailing price, and all buyers to the lowest current market price. In an efficient market the convergence on one price is instant. For discussion see further under Rational pricing.
Purchasing power	Purchasing power is the number of goods/services that can be purchased with a unit of currency. For example, if you had taken one dollar to a store in the 1950s, you would have been able to buy a greater number of items than you would today, indicating that you would have had a greater Purchasing power in the 1950s. Currency can be either a commodity money, like gold or silver, or fiat currency like US dollars.
Purchasing power parity	Purchasing power parity is a theory of long-term equilibrium exchange rates based on relative price levels of two countries. The idea originated with the School of Salamanca in the 16th century and was developed in its modern form by Gustav Cassel in 1918. The concept is founded on the law of one price; the idea that in absence of transaction costs, identical goods will have the same price in different markets. In its `absolute` version, the purchasing power of different currencies is equalized for a given basket of goods.

Open economy	An Open economy is an economy in which there are economic activities between domestic community and outside, e.g. people, including businesses, can trade in goods and services with other people and businesses in the international community, and flow of funds as investment across the border. This contrasts with a closed economy in which international trade and finance cannot take place. The act of selling goods or services to a foreign country is called exporting.
Capital outflow	Capital outflow is an economic term describing capital flowing out of (or leaving) a particular economy. Outflowing capital can be caused by any number of economic or political reasons but can often originate from instability in either sphere. Regardless of cause, Capital outflowing is generally perceived as always undesirable and many countries create laws to restrict the movement of capital out of the nations` borders (called capital controls).

Chapter 6. Unemployment

Natural rate of unemployment	The Natural rate of unemployment is a concept of economic activity developed in particular by Milton Friedman and Edmund Phelps in the 1960s, both recipients of the Nobel prize in economics. In both cases, the development of the concept is cited as a main motivation behind the prize. It represents the hypothetical unemployment rate consistent with aggregate production being at the `long-run` level.
Inflation	In economics, Inflation is a rise in the general level of prices of goods and services in an economy over a period of time. When the price level rises, each unit of currency buys fewer goods and services; consequently, annual Inflation is also an erosion in the purchasing power of money - a loss of real value in the internal medium of exchange and unit of account in the economy. A chief measure of price Inflation is the Inflation rate, the annualized percentage change in a general price index over time.
Inflation rate	In economics, the Inflation rate is a measure of inflation, the rate of increase of a price index . It is the percentage rate of change in price level over time. The rate of decrease in the purchasing power of money is approximately equal. The Inflation rate is used to calculate the real interest rate, as well as real increases in wages, and official measurements of this rate act as input variables to COLA adjustments and inflation derivatives prices.
Recession	In economics, a Recession is a business cycle contraction, a general slowdown in economic activity over a period of time. During Recessions, many macroeconomic indicators vary in a similar way. Production as measured by Gross Domestic Product (GDP), employment, investment spending, capacity utilization, household incomes, business profits and inflation all fall during Recessions; while bankruptcies and the unemployment rate rise.
Stagflation	In economics, the term Stagflation refers to the situation when both the inflation rate and the unemployment rate are high. It is a difficult economic condition for a country, as both inflation and economic stagnation occur simultaneously and no macroeconomic policy can address both of these problems at the same time. The portmanteau Stagflation is generally attributed to British politician Iain Macleod, who coined the term in a speech to Parliament in 1965.
Frictional unemployment	Frictional unemployment involves people in the midst of transiting between jobs, searching for new ones; it is compatible with full employment. It is sometimes called search unemployment and can be voluntary. New entrants (such as graduating students) and re-entrants (such as former homemakers) can also suffer a spell of Frictional unemployment.

Income	Income is the consumption and savings opportunity gained by an entity within a specified time frame, which is generally expressed in monetary terms. However, for households and individuals, \`Income is the sum of all the wages, salaries, profits, interests payments, rents and other forms of earnings received... in a given period of time.\` For firms, Income generally refers to net-profit: what remains of revenue after expenses have been subtracted.
Population growth	In demography, Population growth is used informally for the more specific term Population growth rate , and is often used to refer specifically to the growth of the human population of the world. Simple models of Population growth include the Malthusian Growth Model and the logistic model. In demographics and ecology, Population growth rate (PGR) is the fractional rate at which the number of individuals in a population increases.
Structural unemployment	Structural unemployment is a form of unemployment resulting from a mismatch between the sufficiently skilled workers seeking employment and demand in the labour market. Even though the number of vacancies may be equal to the number of the unemployed, the unemployed workers may lack the skills needed for the jobs -- or may not live in the part of the country or world where the jobs are available. Structural unemployment is a result of the dynamics of the labor market and the fact that these can never be as flexible as, e.g., financial markets.
Fair Labor Standards Act	The Fair Labor Standards Act of 1938 is a United States federal law. It applies to employees engaged in interstate commerce or employed by an enterprise engaged in commerce or in the production of goods for commerce, unless the employer can claim an exemption from coverage. The Fair Labor Standards Act established a national minimum wage, guaranteed \`time-and-a-half\` for overtime in certain jobs, and prohibited most employment of minors in \`oppressive child labor,\` a term defined in the statute.
Current Population Survey	The Current Population Survey is a statistical survey conducted by the United States Census Bureau for the Bureau of Labor Statistics (BLS). The BLS uses the data to provide a monthly report on the Employment Situation. This report provides estimates of the number of unemployed people in the United States.

Earned income tax credit	The United States federal Earned Income Tax Credit is a refundable tax credit; it is means tested, and designed to encourage low-income workers and offset the burden of U.S. payroll taxes. For tax year 2009, a claimant with one qualifying child can receive a maximum credit of $3,043. A claimant with two qualifying children can receive a maximum credit of $5,028. The credit is expanded for tax year 2009 and 2010. For claimants with three or more qualifying children, the maximum credit is $5,657. Grandparents, aunts, uncles, and siblings can also claim a child as their qualifying child provided they shared residence with the child for more than six months of the tax year. However, in tie-breaker situations in which more than one filer claims the same child, priority will be given to the parent.
Gross domestic product	The Gross domestic product or gross domestic income (GDI) is a measure of a country`s overall economic output. It is the market value of all final goods and services made within the borders of a country in a year. It is often positively correlated with the standard of living,; though its use as a stand-in for measuring the standard of living has come under increasing criticism and many countries are actively exploring alternative measures to Gross domestic product for that purpose.
Standard of living	Standard of living is generally measured by standards such as real (i.e. inflation adjusted) income per person and poverty rate. Other measures such as access and quality of health care, income growth inequality and educational standards are also used. Examples are access to certain goods , or measures of health such as life expectancy.
Tax credits	Tax credits may be granted for various types of taxes in recognition of taxes already paid, as a subsidy, or to encourage investment or other behaviors. Tax credits may or may not be refundable to the extent they exceed the respective tax. Tax systems may grant Tax credits to businesses or individuals, and such grants vary by type of credit.
Income tax	An Income tax is a tax levied on the income of individuals or businesses (corporations or other legal entities). Various Income tax systems exist, with varying degrees of tax incidence. Income taxation can be progressive, proportional, or regressive.
Collective bargaining	Collective bargaining is a process between employers and employees to reach an agreement regarding the rights and duties of people at work. Collective bargaining aims to reach a collective agreement which usually sets out issues such as employees pay, working hours, training, health and safety, and rights to participate in workplace or company affairs. During the bargaining process, employees are typically represented by a trade union.

Inventory investment	Inventory investment is a component of gross domestic product (GDP). What is produced in a certain country is naturally also sold eventually, but some of the goods produced in a given year may be sold in a later year rather in the year they are produced. Conversely, some of the goods sold in a given year might have been produced in an earlier year.
Fixed investment	Fixed investment in economics refers to investment in fixed capital, i.e. tangible capital goods , or to the replacement of depreciated capital goods which have been scrapped. Thus, Fixed investment is investment in physical assets such as machinery, land, buildings, installations, vehicles, or technology. Normally, a company balance sheet will state both the amount of expenditure on fixed assets during the quarter or year, and the total value of the stock of fixed assets owned.
Efficiency wage	In labor economics, the efficiency wage hypothesis argues that wages, at least in some markets, are determined by more than simply supply and demand. Specifically, it points to the incentive for managers to pay their employees more than the market-clearing wage in order to increase their productivity or efficiency. This increased labor productivity pays for the higher wages.
Moral hazard	Moral hazard occurs when a party insulated from risk may behave differently than it would behave if it were fully exposed to the risk. Moral hazard is a special case of information asymmetry, a situation in which one party in a transaction has more information than another. The party that is insulated from risk generally has more information about its actions and intentions than the party paying for the negative consequences of the risk.
Taylor rule	A Taylor rule is a monetary-policy rule that stipulates how much the central bank would or should change the nominal interest rate in response to divergences of actual inflation rates from target inflation rates and of actual Gross Domestic Product (GDP) from potential GDP. It was first proposed by the U.S. economist John B. Taylor in 1993.
Real gross domestic product	Real gross domestic product is a macroeconomic measure of the size of an economy adjusted for price changes Gross domestic product is defined as the market value of all final goods and services produced in a geographical region, usually a country. That market value depends on two things: the actual quantity of goods and services produced, and their price. The actual quantity of goods and services produced is sometimes called the volume.

Labor force	In economics, the people in the Labor force are the suppliers of labor. The Labor force is all the nonmilitary people who are officially employed or unemployed. In 2005, the worldwide Labor force was over 3 billion people.
Labor productivity	Labor productivity is the amount of goods and services that a labourer produces in a given amount of time. It is one of several types of productivity that economists measure. Labour productivity can be measured for a firm, a process or a country.
Discouraged worker	In economics, a Discouraged worker is a person of legal employment age who is not actively seeking employment. This is usually because an individual has given up looking or has had no success in finding a job, hence the term `discouraged.` Their belief may derive from a variety of factors including: a shortage of jobs in their locality or line of work; perceived discrimination for reasons such as age, race, sex and religion; a lack of necessary skills, training, or experience; or, a chronic illness or disability. As a general practice, Discouraged workers, who are often classified as `marginally attached to the labor force`, `on the margins` of the labor force, or as part of `hidden unemployment`, are not considered to be part of the labor force and are thus not counted in most official unemployment rates, which influences the appearance and interpretation of unemployment statistics.
Black Death	The Black Death was one of the deadliest pandemics in human history, peaking in Europe between 1348 and 1350. It is widely thought to have been an outbreak of bubonic plague caused by the bacterium Yersinia pestis, but this view has recently been challenged. Usually thought to have started in Central Asia, it had reached the Crimea by 1346. From there, probably carried by fleas residing on the black rats that were regular passengers on merchant ships, it spread throughout the Mediterranean and Europe. The Black Death is estimated to have killed 30% to 60% of Europe`s population, reducing the world`s population from an estimated 450 million to between 350 and 375 million in 1400. This has been seen as creating a series of religious, social and economic upheavals which had profound effects on the course of European history.
Euro	The Euro is the official currency of the Eurozone: 16 of the 27 Member States of the European Union (EU) and is the currency used by the EU institutions. The Eurozone consists of Austria, Belgium, Cyprus, Finland, France, Germany, Greece, Ireland, Italy, Luxembourg, Malta, the Netherlands, Portugal, Slovakia, Slovenia and Spain. Estonia is due to join the Eurozone on 1 January 2011.

Devaluation

Devaluation comes from the word `devalue`, which according to Merriam-Webster means `to lessen the value of.` As such, `Devaluation` is a reduction in the value of a currency with respect to those goods, services or other monetary units with which that currency can be exchanged.

In common modern usage, it specifically implies an official lowering of the value of a country`s currency within a fixed exchange rate system, by which the monetary authority formally sets a new fixed rate with respect to a foreign reference currency. In contrast, depreciation is used for the unofficial decrease in the exchange rate in a floating exchange rate system.

Economic growth

Economic growth is a term used to indicate the increase of per capita gross domestic product (GDP) or other measure of aggregate income. It is often measured as the rate of change in GDP. Economic growth refers only to the quantity of goods and services produced.

Exchange

An exchange is a highly organized market where (especially) tradable securities, commodities, foreign exchange, futures, and options contracts are sold and bought. exchanges bring together brokers and dealers who buy and sell these objects. These various financial instruments can typically be sold either through the exchange, typically with the benefit of a clearinghouse to cover defaults, or over-the-counter, where there is typically less protection against counterparty risk from clearinghouses although OTC clearinghouses have become more common over the years, with regulators placing pressure on the OTC markets to clear and display trades openly.

Exchange rate

In finance, the Exchange rates between two currencies specifies how much one currency is worth in terms of the other. It is the value of a foreign nation`s currency in terms of the home nation`s currency.

Factor price

In economic theory, the price of a finished item affects the factors of production, the various costs and incentives of producing it, so as to `attract` it toward a theoretical Factor price. In other words it is the concept that the price of an item tends to approach the cost of producing it.

There has been much debate as to what determines Factor prices.

Government debt

Government debt is money (or credit) owed by any level of government; either central government, federal government, municipal government or local government. By contrast, annual government deficit refers to the difference between government receipts and spending in a single year. Debt of a sovereign government is called sovereign debt.

Inflation targeting	Inflation targeting is an economic policy in which a central bank estimates and makes public a projected, or `target`, inflation rate and then attempts to steer actual inflation towards the target through the use of interest rate changes and other monetary tools. Because interest rates and the inflation rate tend to be inversely related, the likely moves of the central bank to raise or lower interest rates become more transparent under the policy of Inflation targeting. Examples: · if inflation appears to be above the target, the bank is likely to raise interest rates. This usually (but not always) has the effect over time of cooling the economy and bringing down inflation. · if inflation appears to be below the target, the bank is likely to lower interest rates.
Money	Money is anything that is generally accepted as payment for goods and services and repayment of debts. The main functions of Money are distinguished as: a medium of exchange; a unit of account; a store of value; and, occasionally, a standard of deferred payment. Money originated as commodity Money, but nearly all contemporary Money systems are based on fiat Money.
Economic policy	Economic policy refers to the actions that governments take in the economic field. It covers the systems for setting interest rates and government budget as well as the labour market, national ownership, and many other areas of government interventions into the economy. Such policies are often influenced by international institutions like the International Monetary Fund or World Bank as well as political beliefs and the consequent policies of parties.

Real gross domestic product	Real gross domestic product is a macroeconomic measure of the size of an economy adjusted for price changes Gross domestic product is defined as the market value of all final goods and services produced in a geographical region, usually a country. That market value depends on two things: the actual quantity of goods and services produced, and their price. The actual quantity of goods and services produced is sometimes called the volume.
Gross domestic product	The Gross domestic product or gross domestic income (GDI) is a measure of a country`s overall economic output. It is the market value of all final goods and services made within the borders of a country in a year. It is often positively correlated with the standard of living,; though its use as a stand-in for measuring the standard of living has come under increasing criticism and many countries are actively exploring alternative measures to Gross domestic product for that purpose.
Standard of living	Standard of living is generally measured by standards such as real (i.e. inflation adjusted) income per person and poverty rate. Other measures such as access and quality of health care, income growth inequality and educational standards are also used. Examples are access to certain goods , or measures of health such as life expectancy.
Stagflation	In economics, the term Stagflation refers to the situation when both the inflation rate and the unemployment rate are high. It is a difficult economic condition for a country, as both inflation and economic stagnation occur simultaneously and no macroeconomic policy can address both of these problems at the same time. The portmanteau Stagflation is generally attributed to British politician Iain Macleod, who coined the term in a speech to Parliament in 1965.
Demand	In economics, demand is the desire to own anything and the ability to pay for it and willingness to pay . The term demand signifies the ability or the willingness to buy a particular commodity at a given point of time. Economists record demand on a demand schedule and plot it on a graph as a demand curve that is usually downward sloping.
Good	In economics and accounting, a good is physical product that can be used to satisfy some desire or need. It can be contrasted with a service which is intangible, whereas a good is a tangible physical product, capable of being delivered to a purchaser and involves the transfer of ownership from seller to customer. For example, an apple is a tangible good, as opposed to a haircut, which is an (intangible) service.

Chapter 7. Economic Growth I: Capital Accumulation and Population Growth

Supply and demand	Supply and demand is an economic model of price determination in a market. It concludes that in a competitive market, price will function to equalize the quantity demanded by consumers, and the quantity supplied by producers, resulting in an economic equilibrium of price and quantity. The supply-demand model is a partial equilibrium model representing the determination of the price of a particular good and the quantity of that good which is traded.
Aggregate supply	In economics, Aggregate supply is the total supply of goods and services that firms in a national economy plan on selling during a specific time period. It is the total amount of goods and services that firms are willing to sell at a given price level in an economy. In neo-Keynesian theory seen in many textbooks, an `Aggregate supply and demand` diagram is drawn that looks like a typical Marshallian supply and demand diagram.
Goods and services	In economics, economic output is divided into physical goods and intangible services. Consumption of Goods and services is assumed to produce utility. It is often used when referring to a Goods and services Tax.
Production function	In microeconomics and macroeconomics, a Production function is a function that specifies the output of a firm, an industry, or an entire economy for all combinations of inputs. This function is an assumed technological relationship, based on the current state of engineering knowledge; it does not represent the result of economic choices, but rather is an externally given entity that influences economic decision-making. Almost all economic theories presuppose a Production function, either on the firm level or the aggregate level.
Aggregate Demand-Aggregate Supply model	Aggregate Demand-Aggregate Supply model is a macroeconomic model that explains price level and output through the relationship of aggregate demand and aggregate supply. It was first put forth by John Maynard Keynes in his work The General Theory of Employment, Interest, and Money. It is the foundation for the modern field of macroeconomics, and is accepted by a broad array of economists, from Libertarian, Monetarist supporters of laissez-faire, such as Milton Friedman to Socialist, Post-Keynesian supporters of economic interventionism, such as Joan Robinson.
Consumption	Consumption is a common concept in economics, and gives rise to derived concepts such as consumer debt. Generally, Consumption is defined in part by opposition to production. But the precise definition can vary because different schools of economists define production quite differently.

Consumption function	In economics, the Consumption function is a single mathematical function used to express consumer spending. It was developed by John Maynard Keynes and detailed most famously in his book The General Theory of Employment, Interest, and Money. The function is used to calculate the amount of total consumption in an economy.
Aggregate Demand	In macroeconomics, Aggregate demand is the total demand for final goods and services in the economy (Y) at a given time and price level. It is the amount of goods and services in the economy that will be purchased at all possible price levels. This is the demand for the gross domestic product of a country when inventory levels are static.
Investment	Investment is the commitment of money or capital to purchase financial instruments or other assets in order to gain profitable returns in form of interest, income, or appreciation of the value of the instrument. It is related to saving or deferring consumption. Investment is involved in many areas of the economy, such as business management and finance no matter for households, firms, or governments.
Capital	In economics, capital, capital goods, or real capital are factors of production used to create goods or services that are not themselves significantly consumed (though they may depreciate) in the production process. capital goods may be acquired with money or financial capital. In finance and accounting, capital generally refers to saved-up financial wealth, especially that used to start or maintain a business.
Stock	The Stock or capital Stock of a business entity represents the original capital paid into or invested in the business by its founders. It serves as a security for the creditors of a business since it cannot be withdrawn to the detriment of the creditors. Stock is distinct from the property and the assets of a business which may fluctuate in quantity and value.
Fixed Investment	Fixed investment in economics refers to investment in fixed capital, i.e. tangible capital goods , or to the replacement of depreciated capital goods which have been scrapped. Thus, Fixed investment is investment in physical assets such as machinery, land, buildings, installations, vehicles, or technology. Normally, a company balance sheet will state both the amount of expenditure on fixed assets during the quarter or year, and the total value of the stock of fixed assets owned.

Depreciation

Depreciation is a term used in accounting, economics and finance to spread the cost of an asset over the span of several years. In accounting, however, Depreciation is a term used to describe any method of attributing the historical or purchase cost of an asset across its useful life, roughly corresponding to normal wear and tear.

Steady state

A system in a Steady state has numerous properties that are unchanging in time. This implies that for any property p of the system, the partial derivative with respect to time is zero:

$$\frac{\partial p}{\partial t} = 0$$

The concept of Steady state has relevance in many fields, in particular thermodynamics and economics. Steady state is a more general situation than dynamic equilibrium.

Economic growth

Economic growth is a term used to indicate the increase of per capita gross domestic product (GDP) or other measure of aggregate income. It is often measured as the rate of change in GDP. Economic growth refers only to the quantity of goods and services produced.

Collective bargaining

Collective bargaining is a process between employers and employees to reach an agreement regarding the rights and duties of people at work. Collective bargaining aims to reach a collective agreement which usually sets out issues such as employees pay, working hours, training, health and safety, and rights to participate in workplace or company affairs.

During the bargaining process, employees are typically represented by a trade union.

Exchange

An exchange is a highly organized market where (especially) tradable securities, commodities, foreign exchange, futures, and options contracts are sold and bought. exchanges bring together brokers and dealers who buy and sell these objects. These various financial instruments can typically be sold either through the exchange, typically with the benefit of a clearinghouse to cover defaults, or over-the-counter, where there is typically less protection against counterparty risk from clearinghouses although OTC clearinghouses have become more common over the years, with regulators placing pressure on the OTC markets to clear and display trades openly.

Exchange rate

In finance, the Exchange rates between two currencies specifies how much one currency is worth in terms of the other. It is the value of a foreign nation`s currency in terms of the home nation`s currency.

Income

Income is the consumption and savings opportunity gained by an entity within a specified time frame, which is generally expressed in monetary terms. However, for households and individuals, `Income is the sum of all the wages, salaries, profits, interests payments, rents and other forms of earnings received... in a given period of time.` For firms, Income generally refers to net-profit: what remains of revenue after expenses have been subtracted.

Population growth

In demography, Population growth is used informally for the more specific term Population growth rate , and is often used to refer specifically to the growth of the human population of the world.

Simple models of Population growth include the Malthusian Growth Model and the logistic model.

In demographics and ecology, Population growth rate (PGR) is the fractional rate at which the number of individuals in a population increases.

Inflation

In economics, Inflation is a rise in the general level of prices of goods and services in an economy over a period of time. When the price level rises, each unit of currency buys fewer goods and services; consequently, annual Inflation is also an erosion in the purchasing power of money - a loss of real value in the internal medium of exchange and unit of account in the economy. A chief measure of price Inflation is the Inflation rate, the annualized percentage change in a general price index over time.

Break-even

Break-even is a point where any difference between plus or minus or equivalent changes side.

In economics ' business, specifically cost accounting, the Break-even point (BEP) is the point at which cost or expenses and revenue are equal: there is no net loss or gain, and one has `broken even`. A profit or a loss has not been made, although opportunity costs have been paid, and capital has received the risk-adjusted, expected return.

Interest rate	An Interest rate is the price a borrower pays for the use of money they borrow from a lender, for instance a small company might borrow capital from a bank to buy new assets for their business, and the return a lender receives for deferring the use of funds, by lending it to the borrower. Interests rates are fundamental to a capitalist society. Interest rates are normally expressed as a percentage rate over the period of one year.
Nominal interest rate	In finance and economics Nominal interest rate refers to the rate of interest before adjustment for inflation (in contrast with the real interest rate); or, for interest rates \`as stated\` without adjustment for the full effect of compounding (also referred to as the nominal annual rate). An interest rate is called nominal if the frequency of compounding (e.g. a month) is not identical to the basic time unit (normally a year).
Government debt	Government debt is money (or credit) owed by any level of government; either central government, federal government, municipal government or local government. By contrast, annual government deficit refers to the difference between government receipts and spending in a single year. Debt of a sovereign government is called sovereign debt.

Economic growth	Economic growth is a term used to indicate the increase of per capita gross domestic product (GDP) or other measure of aggregate income. It is often measured as the rate of change in GDP. Economic growth refers only to the quantity of goods and services produced.
Population growth	In demography, Population growth is used informally for the more specific term Population growth rate , and is often used to refer specifically to the growth of the human population of the world. Simple models of Population growth include the Malthusian Growth Model and the logistic model. In demographics and ecology, Population growth rate (PGR) is the fractional rate at which the number of individuals in a population increases.
Capital	In economics, capital, capital goods, or real capital are factors of production used to create goods or services that are not themselves significantly consumed (though they may depreciate) in the production process. capital goods may be acquired with money or financial capital. In finance and accounting, capital generally refers to saved-up financial wealth, especially that used to start or maintain a business.
Steady state	A system in a Steady state has numerous properties that are unchanging in time. This implies that for any property p of the system, the partial derivative with respect to time is zero: $\frac{\partial p}{\partial t} = 0$ The concept of Steady state has relevance in many fields, in particular thermodynamics and economics. Steady state is a more general situation than dynamic equilibrium.
Conditionally convergent	In mathematics, a series or integral is said to be conditionally convergent if it converges, but it does not converge absolutely.

More precisely, a series $\sum_{n=0}^{\infty} a_n$ is said to converge conditionally if $\lim_{m\to\infty} \sum_{n=0}^{m} a_n$ exists and is a finite number (not ∞ or −∞), but $\sum_{n=0}^{\infty} |a_n| = \infty.$

A classical example is given by

$$1 - \frac{1}{2} + \frac{1}{3} - \frac{1}{4} + \frac{1}{5} - \cdots = \sum_{n=1}^{\infty} \frac{(-1)^{n+1}}{n}$$

which converges to $\ln(2)$, but is not absolutely convergent .

The simplest examples of conditionally convergent series (including the one above) are the alternating series.

Factors of production

In economics, Factors of production are the resources employed to produce goods and services. They facilitate production but do not become part of the product (as with raw materials) or become significantly transformed by the production process . To 19th century economists, the Factors of production were land (natural resources, gifts from nature), labor (the ability to work), capital goods (human-made tools and equipment) and enterprise.

Free trade

Free trade is a system of trade policy that allows traders to act and or transact without interference from government. According to the law of comparative advantage the policy permits trading partners mutual gains from trade of goods and services.

Under a Free trade policy, prices are a reflection of true supply and demand, and are the sole determinant of resource allocation.

Adam Smith

Adam Smith was a Scottish moral philosopher and a pioneer of political economics. One of the key figures of the Scottish Enlightenment, Smith is the author of The Theory of Moral Sentiments and An Inquiry into the Nature and Causes of the Wealth of Nations. The latter, usually abbreviated as The Wealth of Nations, is considered his magnum opus and the first modern work of economics.

Endogenous growth theory	In economics, Endogenous growth theory or new growth theory was developed in the 1980s as a response to criticism of the neo-classical growth model. The Endogenous growth theory holds that policy measures can have an impact on the long-run growth rate of an economy. For example, subsidies on research and development or education increase the growth rate in some endogenous growth models by increasing the incentive to innovate.
Instrumental variables	In statistics, econometrics, epidemiology and related disciplines, the method of Instrumental variables is used to estimate causal relationships when controlled experiments are not feasible. Statistically, Instrumental variables methods allow consistent estimation when the explanatory variables (covariates) are correlated with the error terms. Such correlation may occur when the dependent variable causes at least one of the of covariates (`reverse` causation), when there are relevant explanatory variables which are omitted from the model, or when the covariates are subject to measurement error.
Collective bargaining	Collective bargaining is a process between employers and employees to reach an agreement regarding the rights and duties of people at work. Collective bargaining aims to reach a collective agreement which usually sets out issues such as employees pay, working hours, training, health and safety, and rights to participate in workplace or company affairs. During the bargaining process, employees are typically represented by a trade union.
Income	Income is the consumption and savings opportunity gained by an entity within a specified time frame, which is generally expressed in monetary terms. However, for households and individuals, `Income is the sum of all the wages, salaries, profits, interests payments, rents and other forms of earnings received... in a given period of time.` For firms, Income generally refers to net-profit: what remains of revenue after expenses have been subtracted.
Inflation	In economics, Inflation is a rise in the general level of prices of goods and services in an economy over a period of time. When the price level rises, each unit of currency buys fewer goods and services; consequently, annual Inflation is also an erosion in the purchasing power of money - a loss of real value in the internal medium of exchange and unit of account in the economy. A chief measure of price Inflation is the Inflation rate, the annualized percentage change in a general price index over time.

Money	Money is anything that is generally accepted as payment for goods and services and repayment of debts. The main functions of Money are distinguished as: a medium of exchange; a unit of account; a store of value; and, occasionally, a standard of deferred payment. Money originated as commodity Money, but nearly all contemporary Money systems are based on fiat Money.
Budget deficit	A budget deficit occurs when an entity spends more money than it takes in. The opposite of a budget deficit is a budget surplus.
Investment	Investment is the commitment of money or capital to purchase financial instruments or other assets in order to gain profitable returns in form of interest, income, or appreciation of the value of the instrument. It is related to saving or deferring consumption. Investment is involved in many areas of the economy, such as business management and finance no matter for households, firms, or governments.
Surplus	The term surplus is used in economics for several related quantities. The consumer surplus is the amount that consumers benefit by being able to purchase a product for a price that is less than the most that they would be willing to pay. The producer surplus is the amount that producers benefit by selling at a market price mechanism that is higher than the least that they would be willing to sell for.
Human capital	Human capital refers to the stock of competences, knowledge and personality attributes embodied in the ability to perform labor so as to produce economic value. It is the attributes gained by a worker through education and experience. Many early economic theories refer to it simply as workforce, one of three factors of production, and consider it to be a fungible resource -- homogeneous and easily interchangeable.
Growth accounting	Growth accounting is a procedure used in economics to measure the contribution of different factors to economic growth and to indirectly compute the rate of technological progress, measured as a residual, in an economy. This methodology was introduced by Robert Solow in 1957

	Growth accounting decomposes the growth rate of economy`s total output into that which is due to increases in the amount of factors used - usually the increase in the amount of capital and labor - and that which cannot be accounted for by observable changes in factor utilization. The unexplained part of growth in GDP is then taken to represent increases in productivity (getting more output with the same amounts of inputs) or a measure of broadly defined technological progress.
Industrial policy	The Industrial policy `denotes a nation`s declared, official, total strategic effort to influence sectoral development and, thus, national industry portfolio.` These interventionist measures comprise `policies that stimulate specific activities and promote structural change`. Industrial policies are sector specific, unlike broader macroeconomic policies. Examples of horizontal, economywide policies are tightening credit or taxing capital gain, while examples of vertical, sector-specific policies comprise protecting texiles from foreign imports or subsidizing export industries.
Normal goods	In economics, Normal goods are any goods for which demand increases when income increases and falls when income decreases but price remains constant, i.e. with a positive income elasticity of demand. The term does not necessarily refer to the quality of the good. Depending on the indifference curves, the amount of a good bought can either increase, decrease, or stay the same when income increases.
Financial crisis	The term Financial crisis is applied broadly to a variety of situations in which some financial institutions or assets suddenly lose a large part of their value. In the 19th and early 20th centuries, many financial crises were associated with banking panics, and many recessions coincided with these panics. Other situations that are often called financial crises include stock market crashes and the bursting of other financial bubbles, currency crises, and sovereign defaults.
Standard of living	Standard of living is generally measured by standards such as real (i.e. inflation adjusted) income per person and poverty rate. Other measures such as access and quality of health care, income growth inequality and educational standards are also used. Examples are access to certain goods , or measures of health such as life expectancy.

Chapter 8. Economic Growth II: Technology, Empirics, and Policy

Real gross domestic product	Real gross domestic product is a macroeconomic measure of the size of an economy adjusted for price changes Gross domestic product is defined as the market value of all final goods and services produced in a geographical region, usually a country. That market value depends on two things: the actual quantity of goods and services produced, and their price. The actual quantity of goods and services produced is sometimes called the volume.
Economic indicator	An Economic indicator is a statistic about the economy. Economic indicators allow analysis of economic performance and predictions of future performance. One application of Economic indicators is the study of business cycles.
Exchange	An exchange is a highly organized market where (especially) tradable securities, commodities, foreign exchange, futures, and options contracts are sold and bought. exchanges bring together brokers and dealers who buy and sell these objects. These various financial instruments can typically be sold either through the exchange, typically with the benefit of a clearinghouse to cover defaults, or over-the-counter, where there is typically less protection against counterparty risk from clearinghouses although OTC clearinghouses have become more common over the years, with regulators placing pressure on the OTC markets to clear and display trades openly.
Exchange rate	In finance, the Exchange rates between two currencies specifies how much one currency is worth in terms of the other. It is the value of a foreign nation`s currency in terms of the home nation`s currency.
Government debt	Government debt is money (or credit) owed by any level of government; either central government, federal government, municipal government or local government. By contrast, annual government deficit refers to the difference between government receipts and spending in a single year. Debt of a sovereign government is called sovereign debt.
Inflation targeting	Inflation targeting is an economic policy in which a central bank estimates and makes public a projected, or `target`, inflation rate and then attempts to steer actual inflation towards the target through the use of interest rate changes and other monetary tools. Because interest rates and the inflation rate tend to be inversely related, the likely moves of the central bank to raise or lower interest rates become more transparent under the policy of Inflation targeting. Examples:

· if inflation appears to be above the target, the bank is likely to raise interest rates. This usually (but not always) has the effect over time of cooling the economy and bringing down inflation.

· if inflation appears to be below the target, the bank is likely to lower interest rates.

Stagflation

In economics, the term Stagflation refers to the situation when both the inflation rate and the unemployment rate are high. It is a difficult economic condition for a country, as both inflation and economic stagnation occur simultaneously and no macroeconomic policy can address both of these problems at the same time.

The portmanteau Stagflation is generally attributed to British politician Iain Macleod, who coined the term in a speech to Parliament in 1965.

Intellectual property

Intellectual property is a term referring to a number of distinct types of creations of the mind for which property rights are recognised--and the corresponding fields of law. Under Intellectual property law, owners are granted certain exclusive rights to a variety of intangible assets, such as musical, literary, and artistic works; discoveries and inventions; and words, phrases, symbols, and designs. Common types of Intellectual property include copyrights, trademarks, patents, industrial design rights and trade secrets in some jurisdictions.

Labor productivity

Labor productivity is the amount of goods and services that a labourer produces in a given amount of time. It is one of several types of productivity that economists measure. Labour productivity can be measured for a firm, a process or a country.

Total-factor productivity

In economics, total-factor productivity is a variable which accounts for effects in total output not caused by inputs. For example, a year with unusually good weather will tend to have higher output, because bad weather hinders agricultural output. A variable like weather does not directly relate to unit inputs, so weather is considered a total-factor productivity variable.

Property right

A property right is the exclusive authority to determine how a resource is used, whether that resource is owned by government or by individuals. All economic goods have a property rights attribute. This attribute has three broad components

· The right to use the good

· The right to earn income from the good

· The right to transfer the good to others
The concept of property rights as used by economists and legal scholars are related but distinct. The distinction is largely seen in the economists` focus on the ability of an individual or collective to control the use of the good.

Slowdown

A Slowdown is an industrial action in which employees perform their duties but seek to reduce productivity or efficiency in their performance of these duties. A Slowdown may be used as either a prelude or an alternative to a strike, as it is seen as less disruptive as well as less risky and costly for workers and their union. Striking workers usually go unpaid and risk being replaced, so a Slowdown is seen as a way to put pressure on management while avoiding these outcomes.

Bretton Woods system

The Bretton Woods system is commonly understood to refer to the international monetary regime that prevailed from the end of World War II until the early 1970s. Taking its name from the site of the 1944 conference that created the International Monetary Fund (IMF) and World Bank, the Bretton Woods system was history`s first example of a fully negotiated monetary order intended to govern currency relations among sovereign states. In principle, the regime was designed to combine binding legal obligations with multilateral decision-making conducted through an international organization, the IMF, endowed with limited supranational authority.

Depression

In economics, a depression is a sustained, long-term downturn in economic activity in one or more economies. It is a more severe downturn than a recession, which is seen by economists as part of a normal business cycle.

Considered a rare and extreme form of recession, a depression is characterized by its length, and by abnormally large increases in unemployment, falls in the availability of credit-- quite often due to some kind of banking/financial crisis, shrinking output and investment, numerous bankruptcies-- including sovereign debt defaults, significantly reduced amounts of trade and commerce-- especially international, as well as highly volatile relative currency value fluctuations-- most often due to devaluations.

Great Depression

The Great Depression was a severe worldwide economic depression in the decade preceding World War II. The timing of the Great Depression varied across nations, but in most countries it started in about 1929 and lasted until the late 1930s or early 1940s. It was the longest, most widespread, and deepest depression of the 20th century, and is used in the 21st century as an example of how far the world`s economy can decline.

Devaluation

Devaluation comes from the word `devalue`, which according to Merriam-Webster means `to lessen the value of.` As such, `Devaluation` is a reduction in the value of a currency with respect to those goods, services or other monetary units with which that currency can be exchanged.

In common modern usage, it specifically implies an official lowering of the value of a country`s currency within a fixed exchange rate system, by which the monetary authority formally sets a new fixed rate with respect to a foreign reference currency. In contrast, depreciation is used for the unofficial decrease in the exchange rate in a floating exchange rate system.

Microeconomics

Microeconomics is a branch of economics that studies how the individual parts of the economy, the household and the firms, make decisions to allocate limited resources, typically in markets where goods or services are being bought and sold. Microeconomics examines how these decisions and behaviours affect the supply and demand for goods and services, which determines prices, and how prices, in turn, determine the supply and demand of goods and services.

This is a contrast to macroeconomics, which involves the `sum total of economic activity, dealing with the issues of growth, inflation, and unemployment.

Joseph Alois Schumpeter

Joseph Alois Schumpeter was an Austrian economist and political scientist born in Moravia, then part of Austria-Hungary, now in the Czech Republic. He popularized the term `creative destruction` in economics.

Born in TÅ™eÅ¡Å¥, Moravia, Schumpeter began his career studying law at the University of Vienna under the Austrian capital theorist Eugen von Böhm-Bawerk, taking his PhD in 1906. In 1909, after some study trips, he became a professor of economics and government at the University of Czernowitz.

Creative destruction

Creative destruction is an economic theory of innovation and progress, introduced by German sociologist Werner Sombart and elaborated and popularized by the Austrian economist Joseph Schumpeter.

In Capitalism, Socialism and Democracy, Schumpeter popularized and used the term to describe the process of transformation that accompanies radical innovation. In Schumpeter`s vision of capitalism, innovative entry by entrepreneurs was the force that sustained long-term economic growth, even as it destroyed the value of established companies and laborers that enjoyed some degree of monopoly power derived from previous technological, organizational, regulatory, and economic paradigms.

Solow residual

The Solow residual is a number describing empirical productivity growth in an economy from year to year and decade to decade. Robert Solow defined rising productivity as rising output with constant capital and labor input. It is a `residual` because it is the part of growth that cannot be explained through capital accumulation or the accumulation of other traditional factors, such as land or labor.

Four Asian Tigers

The Four Asian Tigers are the highly developed economies of Hong Kong, Singapore, South Korea and Taiwan. These regions were the first newly industrialized countries, noted for maintaining exceptionally high growth rates and rapid industrialization between the early 1960s and 1990s. In the 21st century, all four regions have since graduated into advanced economies and high-income economies. These regions are still the world`s fastest growing industrialized economies. However, attention has increasingly shifted to other Asian economies which are now experiencing faster economic transformation.

Depression	In economics, a depression is a sustained, long-term downturn in economic activity in one or more economies. It is a more severe downturn than a recession, which is seen by economists as part of a normal business cycle. Considered a rare and extreme form of recession, a depression is characterized by its length, and by abnormally large increases in unemployment, falls in the availability of credit-- quite often due to some kind of banking/financial crisis, shrinking output and investment, numerous bankruptcies-- including sovereign debt defaults, significantly reduced amounts of trade and commerce-- especially international, as well as highly volatile relative currency value fluctuations-- most often due to devaluations.
Great Depression	The Great Depression was a severe worldwide economic depression in the decade preceding World War II. The timing of the Great Depression varied across nations, but in most countries it started in about 1929 and lasted until the late 1930s or early 1940s. It was the longest, most widespread, and deepest depression of the 20th century, and is used in the 21st century as an example of how far the world`s economy can decline.
Normal goods	In economics, Normal goods are any goods for which demand increases when income increases and falls when income decreases but price remains constant, i.e. with a positive income elasticity of demand. The term does not necessarily refer to the quality of the good. Depending on the indifference curves, the amount of a good bought can either increase, decrease, or stay the same when income increases.
Recession	In economics, a Recession is a business cycle contraction, a general slowdown in economic activity over a period of time. During Recessions, many macroeconomic indicators vary in a similar way. Production as measured by Gross Domestic Product (GDP), employment, investment spending, capacity utilization, household incomes, business profits and inflation all fall during Recessions; while bankruptcies and the unemployment rate rise.
Government debt	Government debt is money (or credit) owed by any level of government; either central government, federal government, municipal government or local government. By contrast, annual government deficit refers to the difference between government receipts and spending in a single year. Debt of a sovereign government is called sovereign debt.

Chapter 9. Introduction to Economic Fluctuations

Income	Income is the consumption and savings opportunity gained by an entity within a specified time frame, which is generally expressed in monetary terms. However, for households and individuals, \`Income is the sum of all the wages, salaries, profits, interests payments, rents and other forms of earnings received... in a given period of time.\` For firms, Income generally refers to net-profit: what remains of revenue after expenses have been subtracted.
Inflation	In economics, Inflation is a rise in the general level of prices of goods and services in an economy over a period of time. When the price level rises, each unit of currency buys fewer goods and services; consequently, annual Inflation is also an erosion in the purchasing power of money - a loss of real value in the internal medium of exchange and unit of account in the economy. A chief measure of price Inflation is the Inflation rate, the annualized percentage change in a general price index over time.
Inflation rate	In economics, the Inflation rate is a measure of inflation, the rate of increase of a price index . It is the percentage rate of change in price level over time. The rate of decrease in the purchasing power of money is approximately equal. The Inflation rate is used to calculate the real interest rate, as well as real increases in wages, and official measurements of this rate act as input variables to COLA adjustments and inflation derivatives prices.
Investment	Investment is the commitment of money or capital to purchase financial instruments or other assets in order to gain profitable returns in form of interest, income, or appreciation of the value of the instrument. It is related to saving or deferring consumption. Investment is involved in many areas of the economy, such as business management and finance no matter for households, firms, or governments.
Population growth	In demography, Population growth is used informally for the more specific term Population growth rate , and is often used to refer specifically to the growth of the human population of the world. Simple models of Population growth include the Malthusian Growth Model and the logistic model. In demographics and ecology, Population growth rate (PGR) is the fractional rate at which the number of individuals in a population increases.

Stagflation

In economics, the term Stagflation refers to the situation when both the inflation rate and the unemployment rate are high. It is a difficult economic condition for a country, as both inflation and economic stagnation occur simultaneously and no macroeconomic policy can address both of these problems at the same time.

The portmanteau Stagflation is generally attributed to British politician Iain Macleod, who coined the term in a speech to Parliament in 1965.

Business Cycle

The term Business cycle refers to economy-wide fluctuations in production or economic activity over several months or years. These fluctuations occur around a long-term growth trend, and typically involve shifts over time between periods of relatively rapid economic growth (expansion or boom), and periods of relative stagnation or decline (contraction or recession).

These fluctuations are often measured using the growth rate of real gross domestic product.

Real gross domestic product

Real gross domestic product is a macroeconomic measure of the size of an economy adjusted for price changes Gross domestic product is defined as the market value of all final goods and services produced in a geographical region, usually a country. That market value depends on two things: the actual quantity of goods and services produced, and their price. The actual quantity of goods and services produced is sometimes called the volume.

Economic indicator

An Economic indicator is a statistic about the economy. Economic indicators allow analysis of economic performance and predictions of future performance. One application of Economic indicators is the study of business cycles.

Classical dichotomy

In macroeconomics, the Classical dichotomy refers to an idea attributed to classical and pre-Keynesian economics that real and nominal variables can be analyzed separately. To be precise, an economy exhibits the Classical dichotomy if real variables such as output and real interest rates can be completely analyzed without considering what is happening to their nominal counterparts, the money value of output and the interest rate. In particular, this means that real GDP and other real variables can be determined without knowing the level of the nominal money supply or the rate of inflation.

Loanable funds	In economics, the Loanable funds market is a hypothetical market that brings savers and borrowers together, also bringing together the money available in commercial banks and lending institutions available for firms and households to finance expenditures, either investments or consumption. Savers supply the Loanable funds; for instance, buying bonds will transfer their money to the institution issuing the bond, which can be a firm or government. In return, borrowers demand Loanable funds; when an institution sells a bond, it is demanding Loanable funds.
Time horizon	A Time horizon is a fixed point of time in the future at which point certain processes will be evaluated or assumed to end. It is necessary in an accounting, finance or risk management regime to assign such a fixed horizon time so that alternatives can be evaluated for performance over the same period of time. A Time horizon is a physical impossibility in the real world.
Aggregate demand	In macroeconomics, Aggregate demand is the total demand for final goods and services in the economy (Y) at a given time and price level. It is the amount of goods and services in the economy that will be purchased at all possible price levels. This is the demand for the gross domestic product of a country when inventory levels are static.
Consumer price index	A Consumer price index is a measure estimating the average price of consumer goods and services purchased by households. A Consumer price index measures a price change for a constant market basket of goods and services from one period to the next within the same area (city, region, or nation). It is a price index determined by measuring the price of a standard group of goods meant to represent the typical market basket of a typical urban consumer.
Deflation	Deflation is a decrease in the general price level of goods and services. Deflation occurs when the annual inflation rate falls below zero percent (a negative inflation rate), resulting in an increase in the real value of money - allowing one to buy more goods with the same amount of money. This should not be confused with disinflation, a slow-down in the inflation rate.
Hyperinflation	Hyperinflation is inflation that is very high or \`out of control\`, a condition in which prices increase rapidly as a currency loses its value. Definitions used by the media vary from a cumulative inflation rate over three years approaching 100% to \`inflation exceeding 50% a month.\` In informal usage the term is often applied to much lower rates. As a rule of thumb, normal inflation is reported per year, but Hyperinflation is often reported for much shorter intervals, often per month.

Inventory investment	Inventory investment is a component of gross domestic product (GDP). What is produced in a certain country is naturally also sold eventually, but some of the goods produced in a given year may be sold in a later year rather in the year they are produced. Conversely, some of the goods sold in a given year might have been produced in an earlier year.
Fixed investment	Fixed investment in economics refers to investment in fixed capital, i.e. tangible capital goods , or to the replacement of depreciated capital goods which have been scrapped. Thus, Fixed investment is investment in physical assets such as machinery, land, buildings, installations, vehicles, or technology. Normally, a company balance sheet will state both the amount of expenditure on fixed assets during the quarter or year, and the total value of the stock of fixed assets owned.
Aggregate supply	In economics, Aggregate supply is the total supply of goods and services that firms in a national economy plan on selling during a specific time period. It is the total amount of goods and services that firms are willing to sell at a given price level in an economy. In neo-Keynesian theory seen in many textbooks, an `Aggregate supply and demand` diagram is drawn that looks like a typical Marshallian supply and demand diagram.
Economic model	In economics, a model is a theoretical construct that represents economic processes by a set of variables and a set of logical and/or quantitative relationships between them. The Economic model is a simplified framework designed to illustrate complex processes, often but not always using mathematical techniques. Frequently, Economic models use structural parameters.
Long-run	In economic models, the Long-run time frame assumes no fixed factors of production. Firms can enter or leave the marketplace, and the cost (and availability) of land, labor, capital goods and entrepreneurship can be assumed to vary. In contrast, in the short-run time frame, certain factors are assumed to be fixed.
Supply shock	A Supply shock is an event that suddenly changes the price of a commodity or service. It may be caused by a sudden increase or decrease in the supply of a particular good. This sudden change affects the equilibrium price.

Collective bargaining	Collective bargaining is a process between employers and employees to reach an agreement regarding the rights and duties of people at work. Collective bargaining aims to reach a collective agreement which usually sets out issues such as employees pay, working hours, training, health and safety, and rights to participate in workplace or company affairs. During the bargaining process, employees are typically represented by a trade union.
Exchange	An exchange is a highly organized market where (especially) tradable securities, commodities, foreign exchange, futures, and options contracts are sold and bought. exchanges bring together brokers and dealers who buy and sell these objects. These various financial instruments can typically be sold either through the exchange, typically with the benefit of a clearinghouse to cover defaults, or over-the-counter, where there is typically less protection against counterparty risk from clearinghouses although OTC clearinghouses have become more common over the years, with regulators placing pressure on the OTC markets to clear and display trades openly.
Exchange rate	In finance, the Exchange rates between two currencies specifies how much one currency is worth in terms of the other. It is the value of a foreign nation`s currency in terms of the home nation`s currency.
Demand	In economics, demand is the desire to own anything and the ability to pay for it and willingness to pay . The term demand signifies the ability or the willingness to buy a particular commodity at a given point of time. Economists record demand on a demand schedule and plot it on a graph as a demand curve that is usually downward sloping.
Demand shock	In economics, a Demand shock is a sudden event that increases or decreases demand for goods or services temporarily. A positive Demand shock increases demand and a negative Demand shock decreases demand. Prices of goods and services are affected in both cases.
Stabilization policy	A stabilization policy is a package or set of measures introduced to stabilize a financial system or economy. The term can refer to policies in two distinct sets of circumstances: business cycle stabilization and crisis stabilization.

Aggregate Demand-Aggregate Supply model	Aggregate Demand-Aggregate Supply model is a macroeconomic model that explains price level and output through the relationship of aggregate demand and aggregate supply. It was first put forth by John Maynard Keynes in his work The General Theory of Employment, Interest, and Money. It is the foundation for the modern field of macroeconomics, and is accepted by a broad array of economists, from Libertarian, Monetarist supporters of laissez-faire, such as Milton Friedman to Socialist, Post-Keynesian supporters of economic interventionism, such as Joan Robinson.

GDP deflator

In economics, the GDP deflator is a measure of the level of prices of all new, domestically produced, final goods and services in an economy. GDP stands for gross domestic product, the total value of all final goods and services produced within that economy during a specified period.

In most systems of national accounts the GDP deflator measures the ratio of nominal (or current-price) GDP to the real (or chain volume) measure of GDP. The formula used to calculate the deflator is:

$$\text{GDP deflator} = \frac{\text{Nominal GDP}}{\text{Real GDP}} \times 100$$

Dividing the nominal GDP by the GDP deflator and multiplying it by 100 would then give the figure for real GDP, hence deflating the nominal GDP into a real measure.

Central Bank	A Central bank, reserve bank, or monetary authority is a banking institution granted the exclusive privilege to lend a government its currency. Like a normal commercial bank, a Central bank charges interest on the loans made to borrowers, primarily the government of whichever country the bank exists for, and to other commercial banks, typically as a `lender of last resort`. However, a Central bank is distinguished from a normal commercial bank because it has a monopoly on creating the currency of that nation, which is loaned to the government in the form of legal tender.
Monetary policy	Monetary policy is the process by which the central bank or monetary authority of a country controls the supply of money and the rate of interest. Monetary policy is usually used to attain a set of objectives oriented towards the growth and stability of the economy. These goals usually include stable prices and low unemployment.

Chapter 10. Aggregate Demand I: Building the IS-LM Model

John Maynard Keynes	John Maynard Keynes, 1st Baron Keynes, CB was a British economist whose ideas have profoundly affected the theory and practice of modern macroeconomics, as well as the economic policies of governments. He identified the causes of business cycles, and advocated the use of fiscal and monetary measures to mitigate the adverse effects of economic recessions and depressions. His ideas are the basis for the school of thought known as Keynesian economics, and its various offshoots.
Money	Money is anything that is generally accepted as payment for goods and services and repayment of debts. The main functions of Money are distinguished as: a medium of exchange; a unit of account; a store of value; and, occasionally, a standard of deferred payment. Money originated as commodity Money, but nearly all contemporary Money systems are based on fiat Money.
Gross domestic product	The Gross domestic product or gross domestic income (GDI) is a measure of a country`s overall economic output. It is the market value of all final goods and services made within the borders of a country in a year. It is often positively correlated with the standard of living,; though its use as a stand-in for measuring the standard of living has come under increasing criticism and many countries are actively exploring alternative measures to Gross domestic product for that purpose.
Keynesian cross	In the Keynesian cross diagram is a desired total spending (or aggregate expenditure, or `aggregate demand`) curve (shown in blue) is drawn as a rising line since consumers will have a larger demand with a rise in disposable income, which increases with total national output. This increase is due to the positive relationship between consumption and consumers` disposable income in the consumption function. Aggregate demand may also rise due to increases in investment (due to the accelerator effect), while this rise is reduced if imports and tax revenues rise with income. Equilibrium in this diagram occurs where total demand, AD, equals the total amount of national output, Y. Here, total demand equals total supply.
Standard of living	Standard of living is generally measured by standards such as real (i.e. inflation adjusted) income per person and poverty rate. Other measures such as access and quality of health care, income growth inequality and educational standards are also used. Examples are access to certain goods , or measures of health such as life expectancy.
Fiscal policy	In economics, Fiscal policy is the use of government expenditure and revenue collection to influence the economy.

Fiscal policy can be contrasted with the other main type of macroeconomic policy, monetary policy, which attempts to stabilize the economy by controlling interest rates and the supply of money. The two main instruments of Fiscal policy are government expenditure and taxation. Changes in the level and composition of taxation and government spending can impact on the following variables in the economy:

· Aggregate demand and the level of economic activity;

· The pattern of resource allocation;

· The distribution of income

Fiscal policy refers to the use of the government budget to influence the first of these: economic activity.

Government debt

Government debt is money (or credit) owed by any level of government; either central government, federal government, municipal government or local government. By contrast, annual government deficit refers to the difference between government receipts and spending in a single year. Debt of a sovereign government is called sovereign debt.

Interest rate

An Interest rate is the price a borrower pays for the use of money they borrow from a lender, for instance a small company might borrow capital from a bank to buy new assets for their business, and the return a lender receives for deferring the use of funds, by lending it to the borrower. Interests rates are fundamental to a capitalist society. Interest rates are normally expressed as a percentage rate over the period of one year.

Investment

Investment is the commitment of money or capital to purchase financial instruments or other assets in order to gain profitable returns in form of interest, income, or appreciation of the value of the instrument. It is related to saving or deferring consumption. Investment is involved in many areas of the economy, such as business management and finance no matter for households, firms, or governments.

Multiplier

In economics, the multiplier effect or spending multiplier is the idea that an initial amount of spending (usually by the government) leads to increased consumption spending and so results in an increase in national income greater than the initial amount of spending. In other words, an initial change in aggregate demand causes a change in aggregate output for the economy that is a multiple of the initial change.

However, multiplier values less than one have been empirically measured, suggesting that certain types of government spending crowd out private investments and spending that would have otherwise happened.

Tax cut

Economic stimulus via Tax cuts, along with interest rate intervention and deficit spending, are one of the central tenets of Keynesian economics.

The immediate effects of a Tax cut are, generally, a decrease in the real income of the government and an increase in the real income of those whose tax rate has been lowered.

Normal goods

In economics, Normal goods are any goods for which demand increases when income increases and falls when income decreases but price remains constant, i.e. with a positive income elasticity of demand. The term does not necessarily refer to the quality of the good.

Depending on the indifference curves, the amount of a good bought can either increase, decrease, or stay the same when income increases.

Recession

In economics, a Recession is a business cycle contraction, a general slowdown in economic activity over a period of time. During Recessions, many macroeconomic indicators vary in a similar way. Production as measured by Gross Domestic Product (GDP), employment, investment spending, capacity utilization, household incomes, business profits and inflation all fall during Recessions; while bankruptcies and the unemployment rate rise.

Stagflation

In economics, the term Stagflation refers to the situation when both the inflation rate and the unemployment rate are high. It is a difficult economic condition for a country, as both inflation and economic stagnation occur simultaneously and no macroeconomic policy can address both of these problems at the same time.

The portmanteau Stagflation is generally attributed to British politician Iain Macleod, who coined the term in a speech to Parliament in 1965.

Liquidity preference	Liquidity preference in macroeconomic theory refers to the demand for money, considered as liquidity. The concept was first developed by John Maynard Keynes in his book The General Theory of Employment, Interest and Money (1936) to explain determination of the interest rate by the supply and demand for money. The demand for money as an asset was theorized to depend on the interest foregone by not holding bonds.
Demand	In economics, demand is the desire to own anything and the ability to pay for it and willingness to pay . The term demand signifies the ability or the willingness to buy a particular commodity at a given point of time. Economists record demand on a demand schedule and plot it on a graph as a demand curve that is usually downward sloping.
Income	Income is the consumption and savings opportunity gained by an entity within a specified time frame, which is generally expressed in monetary terms. However, for households and individuals, \`Income is the sum of all the wages, salaries, profits, interests payments, rents and other forms of earnings received... in a given period of time.\` For firms, Income generally refers to net-profit: what remains of revenue after expenses have been subtracted.
Aggregate Demand-Aggregate Supply model	Aggregate Demand-Aggregate Supply model is a macroeconomic model that explains price level and output through the relationship of aggregate demand and aggregate supply. It was first put forth by John Maynard Keynes in his work The General Theory of Employment, Interest, and Money. It is the foundation for the modern field of macroeconomics, and is accepted by a broad array of economists, from Libertarian, Monetarist supporters of laissez-faire, such as Milton Friedman to Socialist, Post-Keynesian supporters of economic interventionism, such as Joan Robinson.
Monetary policy	Monetary policy is the process by which the central bank or monetary authority of a country controls the supply of money and the rate of interest. Monetary policy is usually used to attain a set of objectives oriented towards the growth and stability of the economy. These goals usually include stable prices and low unemployment.
Short-run	In economics, the concept of the Short-run refers to the decision-making time frame of a firm in which at least one factor of production is fixed. Costs which are fixed in the Short-run have no impact on a firm decisions. For example a firm can raise output by increasing the amount of labor through overtime.

A generic firm can make three changes in the Short-run:

· Increase production

· Decrease production

· Shut down

In the Short-run, a profit maximizing firm will:

· Increase production if marginal cost is less than price;

· Decrease production if marginal cost is greater than price;

· Continue producing if average variable cost is less than price, even if average total cost is greater than price;

· Shut down if average variable cost is greater than price.

Aggregate Demand-Aggregate Supply model	Aggregate Demand-Aggregate Supply model is a macroeconomic model that explains price level and output through the relationship of aggregate demand and aggregate supply. It was first put forth by John Maynard Keynes in his work The General Theory of Employment, Interest, and Money. It is the foundation for the modern field of macroeconomics, and is accepted by a broad array of economists, from Libertarian, Monetarist supporters of laissez-faire, such as Milton Friedman to Socialist, Post-Keynesian supporters of economic interventionism, such as Joan Robinson.
Short-run	In economics, the concept of the Short-run refers to the decision-making time frame of a firm in which at least one factor of production is fixed. Costs which are fixed in the Short-run have no impact on a firm decisions. For example a firm can raise output by increasing the amount of labor through overtime. A generic firm can make three changes in the Short-run: · Increase production · Decrease production · Shut down In the Short-run, a profit maximizing firm will: · Increase production if marginal cost is less than price; · Decrease production if marginal cost is greater than price; · Continue producing if average variable cost is less than price, even if average total cost is greater than price; · Shut down if average variable cost is greater than price.

Fiscal policy

In economics, Fiscal policy is the use of government expenditure and revenue collection to influence the economy.

Fiscal policy can be contrasted with the other main type of macroeconomic policy, monetary policy, which attempts to stabilize the economy by controlling interest rates and the supply of money. The two main instruments of Fiscal policy are government expenditure and taxation. Changes in the level and composition of taxation and government spending can impact on the following variables in the economy:

· Aggregate demand and the level of economic activity;

· The pattern of resource allocation;

· The distribution of income

Fiscal policy refers to the use of the government budget to influence the first of these: economic activity.

Demand

In economics, demand is the desire to own anything and the ability to pay for it and willingness to pay . The term demand signifies the ability or the willingness to buy a particular commodity at a given point of time.

Economists record demand on a demand schedule and plot it on a graph as a demand curve that is usually downward sloping.

Income

Income is the consumption and savings opportunity gained by an entity within a specified time frame, which is generally expressed in monetary terms. However, for households and individuals, `Income is the sum of all the wages, salaries, profits, interests payments, rents and other forms of earnings received... in a given period of time.` For firms, Income generally refers to net-profit: what remains of revenue after expenses have been subtracted.

Monetary policy

Monetary policy is the process by which the central bank or monetary authority of a country controls the supply of money and the rate of interest. Monetary policy is usually used to attain a set of objectives oriented towards the growth and stability of the economy. These goals usually include stable prices and low unemployment.

Money	Money is anything that is generally accepted as payment for goods and services and repayment of debts. The main functions of Money are distinguished as: a medium of exchange; a unit of account; a store of value; and, occasionally, a standard of deferred payment. Money originated as commodity Money, but nearly all contemporary Money systems are based on fiat Money.
Economic model	In economics, a model is a theoretical construct that represents economic processes by a set of variables and a set of logical and/or quantitative relationships between them. The Economic model is a simplified framework designed to illustrate complex processes, often but not always using mathematical techniques. Frequently, Economic models use structural parameters.
Macroeconomic model	A Macroeconomic model is an analytical tool designed to describe the operation of the economy of a country or a region. These models are usually designed to examine the dynamics of aggregate quantities such as the total amount of goods and services produced, total income earned, the level of employment of productive resources, and the level of prices. Macroeconomic models may be logical, mathematical, and/or computational; the different types of Macroeconomic models serve different purposes and have different advantages and disadvantages.
Government debt	Government debt is money (or credit) owed by any level of government; either central government, federal government, municipal government or local government. By contrast, annual government deficit refers to the difference between government receipts and spending in a single year. Debt of a sovereign government is called sovereign debt.
Investment	Investment is the commitment of money or capital to purchase financial instruments or other assets in order to gain profitable returns in form of interest, income, or appreciation of the value of the instrument. It is related to saving or deferring consumption. Investment is involved in many areas of the economy, such as business management and finance no matter for households, firms, or governments.
Population growth	In demography, Population growth is used informally for the more specific term Population growth rate , and is often used to refer specifically to the growth of the human population of the world.

Simple models of Population growth include the Malthusian Growth Model and the logistic model.

In demographics and ecology, Population growth rate (PGR) is the fractional rate at which the number of individuals in a population increases.

Recession

In economics, a Recession is a business cycle contraction, a general slowdown in economic activity over a period of time. During Recessions, many macroeconomic indicators vary in a similar way. Production as measured by Gross Domestic Product (GDP), employment, investment spending, capacity utilization, household incomes, business profits and inflation all fall during Recessions; while bankruptcies and the unemployment rate rise.

Stock

The Stock or capital Stock of a business entity represents the original capital paid into or invested in the business by its founders. It serves as a security for the creditors of a business since it cannot be withdrawn to the detriment of the creditors. Stock is distinct from the property and the assets of a business which may fluctuate in quantity and value.

Stock market

A Stock market or equity market is a public market for the trading of company stock and derivatives at an agreed price; these are securities listed on a stock exchange as well as those only traded privately.

The size of the world Stock market was estimated at about $36.6 trillion US at the beginning of October 2008. The total world derivatives market has been estimated at about $791 trillion face or nominal value, 11 times the size of the entire world economy. The value of the derivatives market, because it is stated in terms of notional values, cannot be directly compared to a stock or a fixed income security, which traditionally refers to an actual value.

Interest rate

An Interest rate is the price a borrower pays for the use of money they borrow from a lender, for instance a small company might borrow capital from a bank to buy new assets for their business, and the return a lender receives for deferring the use of funds, by lending it to the borrower. Interests rates are fundamental to a capitalist society. Interest rates are normally expressed as a percentage rate over the period of one year.

Stagflation

In economics, the term Stagflation refers to the situation when both the inflation rate and the unemployment rate are high. It is a difficult economic condition for a country, as both inflation and economic stagnation occur simultaneously and no macroeconomic policy can address both of these problems at the same time.

The portmanteau Stagflation is generally attributed to British politician Iain Macleod, who coined the term in a speech to Parliament in 1965.

Accounting scandals

Accounting scandals are political and business scandals which arise with the disclosure of misdeeds by trusted executives of large public corporations. Such misdeeds typically involve complex methods for misusing or misdirecting funds, overstating revenues, understating expenses, overstating the value of corporate assets or underreporting the existence of liabilities, sometimes with the cooperation of officials in other corporations or affiliates.

In public companies, this type of `creative accounting` can amount to fraud and investigations are typically launched by government oversight agencies, such as the Securities and Exchange Commission (SEC) in the United States.

Federal Open Market Committee

The Federal Open Market Committee a component of the Federal Reserve System, is charged under United States law with overseeing the nation`s open market operations. It is the Federal Reserve committee that makes key decisions about interest rates and the growth of the United States money supply. It is the principal organ of United States national monetary policy.

Federal funds

In the United States, Federal funds are overnight borrowings by banks to maintain their bank reserves at the Federal Reserve. Banks keep reserves at Federal Reserve Banks to meet their reserve requirements and to clear financial transactions. Transactions in the Federal funds market enable depository institutions with reserve balances in excess of reserve requirements to lend reserves to institutions with reserve deficiencies.

Federal funds rate

In the United States, the Federal funds rate is the interest rate at which private depository institutions (mostly banks) lend balances (federal funds) at the Federal Reserve to other depository institutions, usually overnight. It is the interest rate banks charge each other for loans.

The interest rate that the borrowing bank pays to the lending bank to borrow the funds is negotiated between the two banks, and the weighted average of this rate across all such transactions is the federal funds effective rate.

Money supply

In economics, Money supply is the total amount of money available in an economy at a particular point in time. There are several ways to define `money,` but standard measures usually include currency in circulation and demand deposits.

Money supply data are recorded and published, usually by the government or the central bank of the country. Public and private-sector analysts have long monitored changes in Money supply because of its possible effects on the price level, inflation and the business cycle.

Open Market

The term Open market is used generally to refer to a situation close to free trade and in a more specific technical sense to interbank trade in securities.

In a general sense used in economics and political economy, an Open market refers to a market which is accessible to all economic actors. In an Open market so defined, all economic actors have an equal opportunity of entry in that market. In banking and financial economics, the Open market is the term used to refer to the environment in which bonds are bought and sold between a central bank & its regulated banks. It is not a free market process.

Aggregate demand

In macroeconomics, Aggregate demand is the total demand for final goods and services in the economy (Y) at a given time and price level. It is the amount of goods and services in the economy that will be purchased at all possible price levels. This is the demand for the gross domestic product of a country when inventory levels are static.

Long-run

In economic models, the Long-run time frame assumes no fixed factors of production. Firms can enter or leave the marketplace, and the cost (and availability) of land, labor, capital goods and entrepreneurship can be assumed to vary. In contrast, in the short-run time frame, certain factors are assumed to be fixed.

Depression

In economics, a depression is a sustained, long-term downturn in economic activity in one or more economies. It is a more severe downturn than a recession, which is seen by economists as part of a normal business cycle.

Considered a rare and extreme form of recession, a depression is characterized by its length, and by abnormally large increases in unemployment, falls in the availability of credit-- quite often due to some kind of banking/financial crisis, shrinking output and investment, numerous bankruptcies-- including sovereign debt defaults, significantly reduced amounts of trade and commerce-- especially international, as well as highly volatile relative currency value fluctuations-- most often due to devaluations.

Great Depression	The Great Depression was a severe worldwide economic depression in the decade preceding World War II. The timing of the Great Depression varied across nations, but in most countries it started in about 1929 and lasted until the late 1930s or early 1940s. It was the longest, most widespread, and deepest depression of the 20th century, and is used in the 21st century as an example of how far the world`s economy can decline.
John Maynard Keynes	John Maynard Keynes, 1st Baron Keynes, CB was a British economist whose ideas have profoundly affected the theory and practice of modern macroeconomics, as well as the economic policies of governments. He identified the causes of business cycles, and advocated the use of fiscal and monetary measures to mitigate the adverse effects of economic recessions and depressions. His ideas are the basis for the school of thought known as Keynesian economics, and its various offshoots.
Revenue	In business, Revenue is income that a company receives from its normal business activities, usually from the sale of goods and services to customers. In many countries, such as the United Kingdom, Revenue is referred to as turnover. Some companies receive Revenue from interest, dividends or royalties paid to them by other companies.
Consumer price index	A Consumer price index is a measure estimating the average price of consumer goods and services purchased by households. A Consumer price index measures a price change for a constant market basket of goods and services from one period to the next within the same area (city, region, or nation). It is a price index determined by measuring the price of a standard group of goods meant to represent the typical market basket of a typical urban consumer.
Deflation	Deflation is a decrease in the general price level of goods and services. Deflation occurs when the annual inflation rate falls below zero percent (a negative inflation rate), resulting in an increase in the real value of money - allowing one to buy more goods with the same amount of money. This should not be confused with disinflation, a slow-down in the inflation rate.
Hyperinflation	Hyperinflation is inflation that is very high or `out of control`, a condition in which prices increase rapidly as a currency loses its value. Definitions used by the media vary from a cumulative inflation rate over three years approaching 100% to `inflation exceeding 50% a month.` In informal usage the term is often applied to much lower rates. As a rule of thumb, normal inflation is reported per year, but Hyperinflation is often reported for much shorter intervals, often per month.

Chapter 11. Aggregate Demand II: Applying the IS-LM Model

Inflation

In economics, Inflation is a rise in the general level of prices of goods and services in an economy over a period of time. When the price level rises, each unit of currency buys fewer goods and services; consequently, annual Inflation is also an erosion in the purchasing power of money - a loss of real value in the internal medium of exchange and unit of account in the economy. A chief measure of price Inflation is the Inflation rate, the annualized percentage change in a general price index over time.

Pigou effect

The Pigou effect is an economics term that refers to the stimulation of output and employment caused by increasing consumption due to a rise in real balances of wealth, particularly during deflation.

Wealth was defined by Arthur Cecil Pigou as the sum of the money supply and government bonds divided by the price level. He argued that Keynes` General theory was deficient in not specifying a link from `real balances` to current consumption and that the inclusion of such a `wealth effect` would make the economy more `self correcting` to drops in aggregate demand than Keynes predicted.

Securitization

Securitization is a structured finance process that distributes risk by aggregating assets in a pool , then issuing new securities backed by the assets and their cash flows. The securities are sold to investors who share the risk and reward from those assets.

Securitization is similar to a sale of a profitable business (`spinning off`) into a separate entity.

Structural unemployment

Structural unemployment is a form of unemployment resulting from a mismatch between the sufficiently skilled workers seeking employment and demand in the labour market. Even though the number of vacancies may be equal to the number of the unemployed, the unemployed workers may lack the skills needed for the jobs -- or may not live in the part of the country or world where the jobs are available.

Structural unemployment is a result of the dynamics of the labor market and the fact that these can never be as flexible as, e.g., financial markets.

Capital

In economics, capital, capital goods, or real capital are factors of production used to create goods or services that are not themselves significantly consumed (though they may depreciate) in the production process. capital goods may be acquired with money or financial capital.

In finance and accounting, capital generally refers to saved-up financial wealth, especially that used to start or maintain a business.

Collective bargaining

Collective bargaining is a process between employers and employees to reach an agreement regarding the rights and duties of people at work. Collective bargaining aims to reach a collective agreement which usually sets out issues such as employees pay, working hours, training, health and safety, and rights to participate in workplace or company affairs.

During the bargaining process, employees are typically represented by a trade union.

Financial crisis

The term Financial crisis is applied broadly to a variety of situations in which some financial institutions or assets suddenly lose a large part of their value. In the 19th and early 20th centuries, many financial crises were associated with banking panics, and many recessions coincided with these panics. Other situations that are often called financial crises include stock market crashes and the bursting of other financial bubbles, currency crises, and sovereign defaults.

Normal goods

In economics, Normal goods are any goods for which demand increases when income increases and falls when income decreases but price remains constant, i.e. with a positive income elasticity of demand. The term does not necessarily refer to the quality of the good.

Depending on the indifference curves, the amount of a good bought can either increase, decrease, or stay the same when income increases.

Liquidity trap

The term Liquidity trap is used in Keynesian economics to refer to a situation where monetary policy is unable to stimulate an economy, either through lowering interest rates or increasing the money supply.

In its original conception, a Liquidity trap resulted when demand for money becomes infinitely elastic (i.e. where the demand curve for money is horizontal) so that further injections of money into the economy will not serve to further lower interest rates. Under the narrow version of Keynesian theory in which this arises, it is specified that monetary policy affects the economy only through its effect on interest rates.

Mundell-Fleming model	The Mundell-Fleming model is an economic model first set forth by Robert Mundell and Marcus Fleming. The model is an extension of the IS-LM model. Whereas the traditional IS-LM Model deals with economy under autarky (or a closed economy), the Mundell-Fleming model tries to describe an open economy.
Good	In economics and accounting, a good is physical product that can be used to satisfy some desire or need. It can be contrasted with a service which is intangible, whereas a good is a tangible physical product, capable of being delivered to a purchaser and involves the transfer of ownership from seller to customer. For example, an apple is a tangible good, as opposed to a haircut, which is an (intangible) service.
Money	Money is anything that is generally accepted as payment for goods and services and repayment of debts. The main functions of Money are distinguished as: a medium of exchange; a unit of account; a store of value; and, occasionally, a standard of deferred payment. Money originated as commodity Money, but nearly all contemporary Money systems are based on fiat Money.
Money market	The Money market is a component of the financial markets for assets involved in short-term borrowing and lending with original maturities of one year or shorter time frames. Trading in the Money markets involves Treasury bills, commercial paper, bankers` acceptances, certificates of deposit, federal funds, and short-lived mortgage- and asset-backed securities. It provides liquidity funding for the global financial system.
Fiscal policy	In economics, Fiscal policy is the use of government expenditure and revenue collection to influence the economy. Fiscal policy can be contrasted with the other main type of macroeconomic policy, monetary policy, which attempts to stabilize the economy by controlling interest rates and the supply of money. The two main instruments of Fiscal policy are government expenditure and taxation. Changes in the level and composition of taxation and government spending can impact on the following variables in the economy: · Aggregate demand and the level of economic activity; · The pattern of resource allocation;

	· The distribution of income Fiscal policy refers to the use of the government budget to influence the first of these: economic activity.
Floating exchange rate	A Floating exchange rate is a type of exchange rate regime wherein a currency`s value is allowed to fluctuate according to the foreign exchange market. A currency that uses a Floating exchange rate is known as a floating currency. It is not possible for a developing country to maintain the stability in the rate of exchange for its currency in the exchange market.
Exchange	An exchange is a highly organized market where (especially) tradable securities, commodities, foreign exchange, futures, and options contracts are sold and bought. exchanges bring together brokers and dealers who buy and sell these objects. These various financial instruments can typically be sold either through the exchange, typically with the benefit of a clearinghouse to cover defaults, or over-the-counter, where there is typically less protection against counterparty risk from clearinghouses although OTC clearinghouses have become more common over the years, with regulators placing pressure on the OTC markets to clear and display trades openly.
Government debt	Government debt is money (or credit) owed by any level of government; either central government, federal government, municipal government or local government. By contrast, annual government deficit refers to the difference between government receipts and spending in a single year. Debt of a sovereign government is called sovereign debt.
Aggregate Demand-Aggregate Supply model	Aggregate Demand-Aggregate Supply model is a macroeconomic model that explains price level and output through the relationship of aggregate demand and aggregate supply. It was first put forth by John Maynard Keynes in his work The General Theory of Employment, Interest, and Money. It is the foundation for the modern field of macroeconomics, and is accepted by a broad array of economists, from Libertarian, Monetarist supporters of laissez-faire, such as Milton Friedman to Socialist, Post-Keynesian supporters of economic interventionism, such as Joan Robinson.
Monetary policy	Monetary policy is the process by which the central bank or monetary authority of a country controls the supply of money and the rate of interest. Monetary policy is usually used to attain a set of objectives oriented towards the growth and stability of the economy. These goals usually include stable prices and low unemployment.

Bretton Woods system	The Bretton Woods system is commonly understood to refer to the international monetary regime that prevailed from the end of World War II until the early 1970s. Taking its name from the site of the 1944 conference that created the International Monetary Fund (IMF) and World Bank, the Bretton Woods system was history`s first example of a fully negotiated monetary order intended to govern currency relations among sovereign states. In principle, the regime was designed to combine binding legal obligations with multilateral decision-making conducted through an international organization, the IMF, endowed with limited supranational authority.
Fixed exchange rate	A Fixed exchange rate is a type of exchange rate regime wherein a currency`s value is matched to the value of another single currency or to a basket of other currencies, or to another measure of value, such as gold. A Fixed exchange rate is usually used to stabilize the value of a currency against the currency it is pegged to. This makes trade and investments between the two countries easier and more predictable, and is especially useful for small economies where external trade forms a large part of their GDP. It can also be used as a means to control inflation.
Appreciation	In accounting, Appreciation of an asset is an increase in its value. In this sense it is the reverse of depreciation, which measures the fall in value of assets over their normal life-time. Generally, the term is reserved for property or, more specifically, land and buildings.
Gold standard	The Gold standard is a monetary system in which the standard economic unit of account is a fixed weight of gold. Three distinct kinds of Gold standard can be identified. The gold specie standard is a system in which the monetary unit is associated with circulating gold coins, or with the unit of value defined in terms of one particular circulating gold coin in conjunction with subsidiary coinage made from a lesser valuable metal.
Depression	In economics, a depression is a sustained, long-term downturn in economic activity in one or more economies. It is a more severe downturn than a recession, which is seen by economists as part of a normal business cycle.

Considered a rare and extreme form of recession, a depression is characterized by its length, and by abnormally large increases in unemployment, falls in the availability of credit-- quite often due to some kind of banking/financial crisis, shrinking output and investment, numerous bankruptcies-- including sovereign debt defaults, significantly reduced amounts of trade and commerce-- especially international, as well as highly volatile relative currency value fluctuations-- most often due to devaluations.

Devaluation

Devaluation comes from the word `devalue`, which according to Merriam-Webster means `to lessen the value of.` As such, `Devaluation` is a reduction in the value of a currency with respect to those goods, services or other monetary units with which that currency can be exchanged.

In common modern usage, it specifically implies an official lowering of the value of a country`s currency within a fixed exchange rate system, by which the monetary authority formally sets a new fixed rate with respect to a foreign reference currency. In contrast, depreciation is used for the unofficial decrease in the exchange rate in a floating exchange rate system.

Great Depression

The Great Depression was a severe worldwide economic depression in the decade preceding World War II. The timing of the Great Depression varied across nations, but in most countries it started in about 1929 and lasted until the late 1930s or early 1940s. It was the longest, most widespread, and deepest depression of the 20th century, and is used in the 21st century as an example of how far the world`s economy can decline.

Normal goods

In economics, Normal goods are any goods for which demand increases when income increases and falls when income decreases but price remains constant, i.e. with a positive income elasticity of demand. The term does not necessarily refer to the quality of the good.

Depending on the indifference curves, the amount of a good bought can either increase, decrease, or stay the same when income increases.

Revaluation

Revaluation means a rise of a price of goods or products. This term is specially used as Revaluation of a currency, where it means a rise of currency to the relation with a foreign currency in a fixed exchange rate. In floating exchange rate correct term would be appreciation.

Surplus

The term surplus is used in economics for several related quantities. The consumer surplus is the amount that consumers benefit by being able to purchase a product for a price that is less than the most that they would be willing to pay. The producer surplus is the amount that producers benefit by selling at a market price mechanism that is higher than the least that they would be willing to sell for.

Chapter 12. The Open Economy Revisited

Collective bargaining	Collective bargaining is a process between employers and employees to reach an agreement regarding the rights and duties of people at work. Collective bargaining aims to reach a collective agreement which usually sets out issues such as employees pay, working hours, training, health and safety, and rights to participate in workplace or company affairs. During the bargaining process, employees are typically represented by a trade union.
Economic growth	Economic growth is a term used to indicate the increase of per capita gross domestic product (GDP) or other measure of aggregate income. It is often measured as the rate of change in GDP. Economic growth refers only to the quantity of goods and services produced.
Economic policy	Economic policy refers to the actions that governments take in the economic field. It covers the systems for setting interest rates and government budget as well as the labour market, national ownership, and many other areas of government interventions into the economy. Such policies are often influenced by international institutions like the International Monetary Fund or World Bank as well as political beliefs and the consequent policies of parties.
Asian financial crisis	The Asian Financial Crisis was a period of financial crisis that gripped much of Asia beginning in July 1997, and raised fears of a worldwide economic meltdown due to financial contagion. The crisis started in Thailand with the financial collapse of the Thai baht caused by the decision of the Thai government to float the baht, cutting its peg to the USD, after exhaustive efforts to support it in the face of a severe financial over extension that was in part real estate driven. At the time, Thailand had acquired a burden of foreign debt that made the country effectively bankrupt even before the collapse of its currency.
Country risk	Country risk refers to the risk of investing in a country, dependent on changes in the business environment that may adversely affect operating profits or the value of assets in a specific country. For example, financial factors such as currency controls, devaluation or regulatory changes, or stability factors such as mass riots, civil war and other potential events contribute to companies` operational risks. This term is also sometimes referred to as political risk, however Country risk is a more general term, which generally only refers to risks affecting all companies operating within a particular country.

Interest rate	An Interest rate is the price a borrower pays for the use of money they borrow from a lender, for instance a small company might borrow capital from a bank to buy new assets for their business, and the return a lender receives for deferring the use of funds, by lending it to the borrower. Interests rates are fundamental to a capitalist society. Interest rates are normally expressed as a percentage rate over the period of one year.
International Monetary Fund	The International Monetary Fund is the international organization that oversees the global financial system by following the macroeconomic policies of its member countries, in particular those with an impact on exchange rate and the balance of payments. It is an organization formed with a stated objective of stabilizing international exchange rates and facilitating development through the enforcement of liberalising economic policies on other countries as a condition for loans, restructuring or aid. It also offers highly leveraged loans, mainly to poorer countries.
Inflation	In economics, Inflation is a rise in the general level of prices of goods and services in an economy over a period of time. When the price level rises, each unit of currency buys fewer goods and services; consequently, annual Inflation is also an erosion in the purchasing power of money - a loss of real value in the internal medium of exchange and unit of account in the economy. A chief measure of price Inflation is the Inflation rate, the annualized percentage change in a general price index over time.
Investment	Investment is the commitment of money or capital to purchase financial instruments or other assets in order to gain profitable returns in form of interest, income, or appreciation of the value of the instrument. It is related to saving or deferring consumption. Investment is involved in many areas of the economy, such as business management and finance no matter for households, firms, or governments.
Euro	The Euro is the official currency of the Eurozone: 16 of the 27 Member States of the European Union (EU) and is the currency used by the EU institutions. The Eurozone consists of Austria, Belgium, Cyprus, Finland, France, Germany, Greece, Ireland, Italy, Luxembourg, Malta, the Netherlands, Portugal, Slovakia, Slovenia and Spain. Estonia is due to join the Eurozone on 1 January 2011.
Dollarization	Dollarization occurs when the inhabitants of a country use foreign currency in parallel to or instead of the domestic currency. The term is not only applied to usage of the United States dollar, but generally to the use of any foreign currency as the national currency.

Official Dollarization has gained prominence as several countries have considered and implemented it as official policy. The major advantage of Dollarization is promoting fiscal discipline and thus greater financial stability and lower inflation.

Impossible trinity

The Impossible trinity is the Trilemma in international economics suggesting it is impossible to have all three of the following at the same time:

· A fixed exchange rate.

· Free capital movement (absence of capital controls).

· An independent monetary policy.

It is both a hypotheis based on IS/LM models that have been extended to include a BOP component, and a finding from empirical examples where governments which have tried to simultaneously pursue all three goals have always failed.

The formal model for this hypothesis is the Mundell-Fleming model developed in the 1960s by Robert Mundell and Marcus Fleming.

Speculative attack

A Speculative attack is the massive selling of a country`s currency assets by both domestic and foreign investors. Countries that utilize a fixed exchange rate are more susceptible to a Speculative attack than countries utilizing a floating exchange rate. This is because of the large amount of reserves necessary to hold the fixed exchange rate in place at that fixed level.

Central bank

A Central bank, reserve bank, or monetary authority is a banking institution granted the exclusive privilege to lend a government its currency. Like a normal commercial bank, a Central bank charges interest on the loans made to borrowers, primarily the government of whichever country the bank exists for, and to other commercial banks, typically as a `lender of last resort`. However, a Central bank is distinguished from a normal commercial bank because it has a monopoly on creating the currency of that nation, which is loaned to the government in the form of legal tender.

Price level

A Price level is a hypothetical measure of overall prices for some set of goods and services, in a given region during a given interval, normalized relative to some base set. Typically, a Price level is approximated with a price index.

Income

Income is the consumption and savings opportunity gained by an entity within a specified time frame, which is generally expressed in monetary terms. However, for households and individuals, `Income is the sum of all the wages, salaries, profits, interests payments, rents and other forms of earnings received... in a given period of time.` For firms, Income generally refers to net-profit: what remains of revenue after expenses have been subtracted.

Population growth

In demography, Population growth is used informally for the more specific term Population growth rate , and is often used to refer specifically to the growth of the human population of the world.

Simple models of Population growth include the Malthusian Growth Model and the logistic model.

In demographics and ecology, Population growth rate (PGR) is the fractional rate at which the number of individuals in a population increases.

Short-run

In economics, the concept of the Short-run refers to the decision-making time frame of a firm in which at least one factor of production is fixed. Costs which are fixed in the Short-run have no impact on a firm decisions. For example a firm can raise output by increasing the amount of labor through overtime.

A generic firm can make three changes in the Short-run:

· Increase production

· Decrease production

· Shut down

In the Short-run, a profit maximizing firm will:

· Increase production if marginal cost is less than price;

· Decrease production if marginal cost is greater than price;

· Continue producing if average variable cost is less than price, even if average total cost is greater than price;

· Shut down if average variable cost is greater than price.

Aggregate supply	In economics, Aggregate supply is the total supply of goods and services that firms in a national economy plan on selling during a specific time period. It is the total amount of goods and services that firms are willing to sell at a given price level in an economy. In neo-Keynesian theory seen in many textbooks, an `Aggregate supply and demand` diagram is drawn that looks like a typical Marshallian supply and demand diagram.
Phillips curve	In economics, the Phillips curve is a historical inverse relationship between the rate of unemployment and the rate of inflation in an economy. Stated simply, the lower the unemployment in an economy, the higher the rate of increase in nominal wages. While it has been observed that there is a stable short run tradeoff between unemployment and inflation this has not been observed in the long run.
Aggregate Demand-Aggregate Supply model	Aggregate Demand-Aggregate Supply model is a macroeconomic model that explains price level and output through the relationship of aggregate demand and aggregate supply. It was first put forth by John Maynard Keynes in his work The General Theory of Employment, Interest, and Money. It is the foundation for the modern field of macroeconomics, and is accepted by a broad array of economists, from Libertarian, Monetarist supporters of laissez-faire, such as Milton Friedman to Socialist, Post-Keynesian supporters of economic interventionism, such as Joan Robinson.
Deflation	Deflation is a decrease in the general price level of goods and services. Deflation occurs when the annual inflation rate falls below zero percent (a negative inflation rate), resulting in an increase in the real value of money - allowing one to buy more goods with the same amount of money. This should not be confused with disinflation, a slow-down in the inflation rate.
Hyperinflation	Hyperinflation is inflation that is very high or `out of control`, a condition in which prices increase rapidly as a currency loses its value. Definitions used by the media vary from a cumulative inflation rate over three years approaching 100% to `inflation exceeding 50% a month.` In informal usage the term is often applied to much lower rates. As a rule of thumb, normal inflation is reported per year, but Hyperinflation is often reported for much shorter intervals, often per month.
NAIRU	In monetarist economics, particularly the work of Milton Friedman, NAIRU and refers to a level of unemployment below which inflation rises. It is widely used in mainstream economics, but is rejected by other economists such as James Tobin - and, in earlier forms, by John Maynard Keynes - who argue that literal full employment - a rate of unemployment close to 0% - is natural and attainable.

An early form of NAIRU is found in the work of Abba P. Lerner (Lerner 1951, Chapter 14), who referred to it as `low full employment`, to contrast with the `high full employment` achievable under his theory of functional finance.

Adaptive expectations

In economics, Adaptive expectations means that people form their expectations about what will happen in the future based on what has happened in the past. For example, if inflation has been higher than expected in the past, people would revise expectations for the future.

One simple version of Adaptive expectations is stated in the following equation, where p^e is the next year`s rate of inflation that is currently expected; $p^e_{-1}$ is this year`s rate of inflation that was expected last year; and p is this year`s actual rate of inflation:

$$p^e = p^e_{-1} + \lambda(p_{-1} - p^e_{-1})$$

With λ is between 0 and 1, this says that current expectations of future inflation reflect past expectations and an `error-adjustment` term, in which current expectations are raised (or lowered) according to the gap between actual inflation and previous expectations.

Inflation rate

In economics, the Inflation rate is a measure of inflation, the rate of increase of a price index . It is the percentage rate of change in price level over time. The rate of decrease in the purchasing power of money is approximately equal. The Inflation rate is used to calculate the real interest rate, as well as real increases in wages, and official measurements of this rate act as input variables to COLA adjustments and inflation derivatives prices.

Standard of living

Standard of living is generally measured by standards such as real (i.e. inflation adjusted) income per person and poverty rate. Other measures such as access and quality of health care, income growth inequality and educational standards are also used. Examples are access to certain goods , or measures of health such as life expectancy.

Cost-push inflation

Cost-push inflation is a type of inflation caused by substantial increases in the cost of important goods or services where no suitable alternative is available. A situation that has been often cited of this was the oil crisis of the 1970s, which some economists see as a major cause of the inflation experienced in the Western world in that decade. It is argued that this inflation resulted from increases in the cost of petroleum imposed by the member states of OPEC. Since petroleum is so important to industrialised economies, a large increase in its price can lead to the increase in the price of most products, raising the inflation rate.

Demand-pull inflation	Demand-pull inflation arises when aggregate demand in an economy outpaces aggregate supply. It involves inflation rising as real gross domestic product rises and unemployment falls, as the economy moves along the Phillips curve. This is commonly described as `too much money chasing too few goods`.
Real gross domestic product	Real gross domestic product is a macroeconomic measure of the size of an economy adjusted for price changes Gross domestic product is defined as the market value of all final goods and services produced in a geographical region, usually a country. That market value depends on two things: the actual quantity of goods and services produced, and their price. The actual quantity of goods and services produced is sometimes called the volume.
Interest rate	An Interest rate is the price a borrower pays for the use of money they borrow from a lender, for instance a small company might borrow capital from a bank to buy new assets for their business, and the return a lender receives for deferring the use of funds, by lending it to the borrower. Interests rates are fundamental to a capitalist society. Interest rates are normally expressed as a percentage rate over the period of one year.
Money	Money is anything that is generally accepted as payment for goods and services and repayment of debts. The main functions of Money are distinguished as: a medium of exchange; a unit of account; a store of value; and, occasionally, a standard of deferred payment. Money originated as commodity Money, but nearly all contemporary Money systems are based on fiat Money.
Nominal interest rate	In finance and economics Nominal interest rate refers to the rate of interest before adjustment for inflation (in contrast with the real interest rate); or, for interest rates `as stated` without adjustment for the full effect of compounding (also referred to as the nominal annual rate). An interest rate is called nominal if the frequency of compounding (e.g. a month) is not identical to the basic time unit (normally a year).
Stagflation	In economics, the term Stagflation refers to the situation when both the inflation rate and the unemployment rate are high. It is a difficult economic condition for a country, as both inflation and economic stagnation occur simultaneously and no macroeconomic policy can address both of these problems at the same time. The portmanteau Stagflation is generally attributed to British politician Iain Macleod, who coined the term in a speech to Parliament in 1965.

Recession	In economics, a Recession is a business cycle contraction, a general slowdown in economic activity over a period of time. During Recessions, many macroeconomic indicators vary in a similar way. Production as measured by Gross Domestic Product (GDP), employment, investment spending, capacity utilization, household incomes, business profits and inflation all fall during Recessions; while bankruptcies and the unemployment rate rise.
Vietnam War	The Vietnam War was a Cold War military conflict that occurred in Vietnam, Laos, and Cambodia from November 1, 1955 , to April 30, 1975 when Saigon fell. This war followed the First Indochina War and was fought between the communist North Vietnam, supported by its communist allies, and the government of South Vietnam, supported by the United States and other anti-communist nations. The Viet Cong, a lightly-armed South Vietnamese communist-controlled common front, largely fought a guerrilla war against anti-communist forces in the region.
Aggregate demand	In macroeconomics, Aggregate demand is the total demand for final goods and services in the economy (Y) at a given time and price level. It is the amount of goods and services in the economy that will be purchased at all possible price levels. This is the demand for the gross domestic product of a country when inventory levels are static.
Investment	Investment is the commitment of money or capital to purchase financial instruments or other assets in order to gain profitable returns in form of interest, income, or appreciation of the value of the instrument. It is related to saving or deferring consumption. Investment is involved in many areas of the economy, such as business management and finance no matter for households, firms, or governments.
Population growth	In demography, Population growth is used informally for the more specific term Population growth rate , and is often used to refer specifically to the growth of the human population of the world. Simple models of Population growth include the Malthusian Growth Model and the logistic model. In demographics and ecology, Population growth rate (PGR) is the fractional rate at which the number of individuals in a population increases.

Price control

Price controls are governmental impositions on the prices charged for goods and services in a market, usually intended to maintain the affordability of staple foods and goods, and to prevent price gouging during shortages, or, alternately, to insure an income for providers of certain goods. There are two primary forms of Price control, a price ceiling, the maximum price that can be charged, and a price floor, the minimum price that can be charged.

Historically, Price controls have often been imposed as part of a larger incomes policy package also employing wage controls and other regulatory elements.

Short-run

In economics, the concept of the Short-run refers to the decision-making time frame of a firm in which at least one factor of production is fixed. Costs which are fixed in the Short-run have no impact on a firm decisions. For example a firm can raise output by increasing the amount of labor through overtime.

A generic firm can make three changes in the Short-run:

· Increase production

· Decrease production

· Shut down

In the Short-run, a profit maximizing firm will:

· Increase production if marginal cost is less than price;

· Decrease production if marginal cost is greater than price;

· Continue producing if average variable cost is less than price, even if average total cost is greater than price;

· Shut down if average variable cost is greater than price.

Financial crisis	The term Financial crisis is applied broadly to a variety of situations in which some financial institutions or assets suddenly lose a large part of their value. In the 19th and early 20th centuries, many financial crises were associated with banking panics, and many recessions coincided with these panics. Other situations that are often called financial crises include stock market crashes and the bursting of other financial bubbles, currency crises, and sovereign defaults.
Stock	The Stock or capital Stock of a business entity represents the original capital paid into or invested in the business by its founders. It serves as a security for the creditors of a business since it cannot be withdrawn to the detriment of the creditors. Stock is distinct from the property and the assets of a business which may fluctuate in quantity and value.
Disinflation	Disinflation is a decrease in the rate of inflation - a slowdown in the rate of increase of the general price level of goods and services in a nation`s gross domestic product over time. It is the opposite of reflation. If the inflation rate is not very high to start with, Disinflation can lead to deflation - decreases in the general price level of goods and services.
Rational expectations	Rational expectations is a hypothesis in economics which states that agents` predictions of the future value of economically relevant variables, is not systematically wrong in that all errors are random. An alternative formulation is that Rational expectations are model-consistent expectations, in that the agents inside the model assume the model`s predictions are valid. The Rational expectations assumption is used in many contemporary macroeconomic models, game theory and other applications of rational choice theory.
Economic model	In economics, a model is a theoretical construct that represents economic processes by a set of variables and a set of logical and/or quantitative relationships between them. The Economic model is a simplified framework designed to illustrate complex processes, often but not always using mathematical techniques. Frequently, Economic models use structural parameters.

Aggregate Demand-Aggregate Supply model	Aggregate Demand-Aggregate Supply model is a macroeconomic model that explains price level and output through the relationship of aggregate demand and aggregate supply. It was first put forth by John Maynard Keynes in his work The General Theory of Employment, Interest, and Money. It is the foundation for the modern field of macroeconomics, and is accepted by a broad array of economists, from Libertarian, Monetarist supporters of laissez-faire, such as Milton Friedman to Socialist, Post-Keynesian supporters of economic interventionism, such as Joan Robinson.
Demand	In economics, demand is the desire to own anything and the ability to pay for it and willingness to pay . The term demand signifies the ability or the willingness to buy a particular commodity at a given point of time. Economists record demand on a demand schedule and plot it on a graph as a demand curve that is usually downward sloping.
Gross domestic product	The Gross domestic product or gross domestic income (GDI) is a measure of a country`s overall economic output. It is the market value of all final goods and services made within the borders of a country in a year. It is often positively correlated with the standard of living,; though its use as a stand-in for measuring the standard of living has come under increasing criticism and many countries are actively exploring alternative measures to Gross domestic product for that purpose.
Income	Income is the consumption and savings opportunity gained by an entity within a specified time frame, which is generally expressed in monetary terms. However, for households and individuals, `Income is the sum of all the wages, salaries, profits, interests payments, rents and other forms of earnings received... in a given period of time.` For firms, Income generally refers to net-profit: what remains of revenue after expenses have been subtracted.
Fisher equation	The Fisher equation in financial mathematics and economics estimates the relationship between nominal and real interest rates under inflation. It is named after Irving Fisher who was famous for his works on the theory of interest. In finance, the Fisher equation is primarily used in YTM calculations of bonds or IRR calculations of investments. In economics, this equation is used to predict nominal and real interest rate behavior.
Phillips curve	In economics, the Phillips curve is a historical inverse relationship between the rate of unemployment and the rate of inflation in an economy. Stated simply, the lower the unemployment in an economy, the higher the rate of increase in nominal wages. While it has been observed that there is a stable short run tradeoff between unemployment and inflation this has not been observed in the long run.

Real interest rate

The Real interest rate is approximately the nominal interest rate minus the inflation rate. It is the rate of interest an investor expects to receive after subtracting inflation. This is not a single number, as different investors have different expectations of future inflation. If, for example, an investor were able to lock in a 5% interest rate for the coming year and anticipated a 2% rise in prices, it would expect to earn a Real interest rate of 3%.

Deflation

Deflation is a decrease in the general price level of goods and services. Deflation occurs when the annual inflation rate falls below zero percent (a negative inflation rate), resulting in an increase in the real value of money - allowing one to buy more goods with the same amount of money. This should not be confused with disinflation, a slow-down in the inflation rate.

Hyperinflation

Hyperinflation is inflation that is very high or `out of control`, a condition in which prices increase rapidly as a currency loses its value. Definitions used by the media vary from a cumulative inflation rate over three years approaching 100% to `inflation exceeding 50% a month.` In informal usage the term is often applied to much lower rates. As a rule of thumb, normal inflation is reported per year, but Hyperinflation is often reported for much shorter intervals, often per month.

Adaptive expectations

In economics, Adaptive expectations means that people form their expectations about what will happen in the future based on what has happened in the past. For example, if inflation has been higher than expected in the past, people would revise expectations for the future.

One simple version of Adaptive expectations is stated in the following equation, where p^e is the next year`s rate of inflation that is currently expected; $p^e_{-1}$ is this year`s rate of inflation that was expected last year; and p is this year`s actual rate of inflation:

$$p^e = p^e_{-1} + \lambda(p_{-1} - p^e_{-1})$$

With λ is between 0 and 1, this says that current expectations of future inflation reflect past expectations and an `error-adjustment` term, in which current expectations are raised (or lowered) according to the gap between actual inflation and previous expectations.

Federal Open Market Committee

The Federal Open Market Committee a component of the Federal Reserve System, is charged under United States law with overseeing the nation`s open market operations. It is the Federal Reserve committee that makes key decisions about interest rates and the growth of the United States money supply. It is the principal organ of United States national monetary policy.

Open Market

The term Open market is used generally to refer to a situation close to free trade and in a more specific technical sense to interbank trade in securities.

In a general sense used in economics and political economy, an Open market refers to a market which is accessible to all economic actors. In an Open market so defined, all economic actors have an equal opportunity of entry in that market. In banking and financial economics, the Open market is the term used to refer to the environment in which bonds are bought and sold between a central bank & its regulated banks. It is not a free market process.

Taylor rule

A Taylor rule is a monetary-policy rule that stipulates how much the central bank would or should change the nominal interest rate in response to divergences of actual inflation rates from target inflation rates and of actual Gross Domestic Product (GDP) from potential GDP. It was first proposed by the U.S. economist John B. Taylor in 1993.

Federal funds

In the United States, Federal funds are overnight borrowings by banks to maintain their bank reserves at the Federal Reserve. Banks keep reserves at Federal Reserve Banks to meet their reserve requirements and to clear financial transactions. Transactions in the Federal funds market enable depository institutions with reserve balances in excess of reserve requirements to lend reserves to institutions with reserve deficiencies.

Federal funds rate

In the United States, the Federal funds rate is the interest rate at which private depository institutions (mostly banks) lend balances (federal funds) at the Federal Reserve to other depository institutions, usually overnight. It is the interest rate banks charge each other for loans.

The interest rate that the borrowing bank pays to the lending bank to borrow the funds is negotiated between the two banks, and the weighted average of this rate across all such transactions is the federal funds effective rate.

Short-run

In economics, the concept of the Short-run refers to the decision-making time frame of a firm in which at least one factor of production is fixed. Costs which are fixed in the Short-run have no impact on a firm decisions. For example a firm can raise output by increasing the amount of labor through overtime.

A generic firm can make three changes in the Short-run:

· Increase production

· Decrease production

· Shut down

In the Short-run, a profit maximizing firm will:

· Increase production if marginal cost is less than price;

· Decrease production if marginal cost is greater than price;

· Continue producing if average variable cost is less than price, even if average total cost is greater than price;

· Shut down if average variable cost is greater than price.

Aggregate supply

In economics, Aggregate supply is the total supply of goods and services that firms in a national economy plan on selling during a specific time period. It is the total amount of goods and services that firms are willing to sell at a given price level in an economy.

In neo-Keynesian theory seen in many textbooks, an `Aggregate supply and demand` diagram is drawn that looks like a typical Marshallian supply and demand diagram.

Long-run

In economic models, the Long-run time frame assumes no fixed factors of production. Firms can enter or leave the marketplace, and the cost (and availability) of land, labor, capital goods and entrepreneurship can be assumed to vary. In contrast, in the short-run time frame, certain factors are assumed to be fixed.

Aggregate demand

In macroeconomics, Aggregate demand is the total demand for final goods and services in the economy (Y) at a given time and price level. It is the amount of goods and services in the economy that will be purchased at all possible price levels. This is the demand for the gross domestic product of a country when inventory levels are static.

Demand curve	In economics, the Demand curve is the graph depicting the relationship between the price of a certain commodity, and the amount of it that consumers are willing and able to purchase at that given price. It is a graphic representation of a demand schedule. The Demand curve for all consumers together follows from the Demand curve of every individual consumer: the individual demands at each price are added together.
Economic growth	Economic growth is a term used to indicate the increase of per capita gross domestic product (GDP) or other measure of aggregate income. It is often measured as the rate of change in GDP. Economic growth refers only to the quantity of goods and services produced.
Stagflation	In economics, the term Stagflation refers to the situation when both the inflation rate and the unemployment rate are high. It is a difficult economic condition for a country, as both inflation and economic stagnation occur simultaneously and no macroeconomic policy can address both of these problems at the same time. The portmanteau Stagflation is generally attributed to British politician Iain Macleod, who coined the term in a speech to Parliament in 1965.
Monetary policy	Monetary policy is the process by which the central bank or monetary authority of a country controls the supply of money and the rate of interest. Monetary policy is usually used to attain a set of objectives oriented towards the growth and stability of the economy. These goals usually include stable prices and low unemployment.
Central Bank	A Central bank, reserve bank, or monetary authority is a banking institution granted the exclusive privilege to lend a government its currency. Like a normal commercial bank, a Central bank charges interest on the loans made to borrowers, primarily the government of whichever country the bank exists for, and to other commercial banks, typically as a `lender of last resort`. However, a Central bank is distinguished from a normal commercial bank because it has a monopoly on creating the currency of that nation, which is loaned to the government in the form of legal tender.
Federal Reserve System	The Federal Reserve System is the central banking system of the United States. It was created in 1913 with the enactment of the Federal Reserve Act, and was largely a response to a series of financial panics, particularly a severe panic in 1907. Over time, the roles and responsibilities of the Federal Reserve System have expanded and its structure has evolved.

Real gross domestic product	Real gross domestic product is a macroeconomic measure of the size of an economy adjusted for price changes Gross domestic product is defined as the market value of all final goods and services produced in a geographical region, usually a country. That market value depends on two things: the actual quantity of goods and services produced, and their price. The actual quantity of goods and services produced is sometimes called the volume.
Money	Money is anything that is generally accepted as payment for goods and services and repayment of debts. The main functions of Money are distinguished as: a medium of exchange; a unit of account; a store of value; and, occasionally, a standard of deferred payment. Money originated as commodity Money, but nearly all contemporary Money systems are based on fiat Money.
Nominal interest rate	In finance and economics Nominal interest rate refers to the rate of interest before adjustment for inflation (in contrast with the real interest rate); or, for interest rates `as stated` without adjustment for the full effect of compounding (also referred to as the nominal annual rate). An interest rate is called nominal if the frequency of compounding (e.g. a month) is not identical to the basic time unit (normally a year).
Investment	Investment is the commitment of money or capital to purchase financial instruments or other assets in order to gain profitable returns in form of interest, income, or appreciation of the value of the instrument. It is related to saving or deferring consumption. Investment is involved in many areas of the economy, such as business management and finance no matter for households, firms, or governments.

Chapter 15. Stabilization Policy

Stabilization policy	A stabilization policy is a package or set of measures introduced to stabilize a financial system or economy. The term can refer to policies in two distinct sets of circumstances: business cycle stabilization and crisis stabilization.
Council of Economic Advisers	The Council of Economic Advisers is a group of three economists who advise the President of the United States on economic policy. It is a part of the Executive Office of the President of the United States, and provides much of the economic policy of the White House. The council prepares the annual Economic Report of the President.
Federal Reserve System	The Federal Reserve System is the central banking system of the United States. It was created in 1913 with the enactment of the Federal Reserve Act, and was largely a response to a series of financial panics, particularly a severe panic in 1907. Over time, the roles and responsibilities of the Federal Reserve System have expanded and its structure has evolved.
Investment	Investment is the commitment of money or capital to purchase financial instruments or other assets in order to gain profitable returns in form of interest, income, or appreciation of the value of the instrument. It is related to saving or deferring consumption. Investment is involved in many areas of the economy, such as business management and finance no matter for households, firms, or governments.
Economic policy	Economic policy refers to the actions that governments take in the economic field. It covers the systems for setting interest rates and government budget as well as the labour market, national ownership, and many other areas of government interventions into the economy. Such policies are often influenced by international institutions like the International Monetary Fund or World Bank as well as political beliefs and the consequent policies of parties.
Inside lag	In economics, an Inside lag is the amount of time it takes for a government or a central bank to respond to a shock in the economy. It is the delay in implementation of a monetary policy. Its converse is outside lag (the amount of time before an action by a government or a central bank affects an economy).
Outside lag	In economics, an Outside lag is the amount of time it takes for a government or central bank`s actions, in the form of either monetary or fiscal policy, to have a visible effect on the economy. Its converse is inside lag.

Automatic stabilizers

In macroeconomics automatic stabilizers work as a tool to dampen fluctuations in real GDP without any explicit policy action by the government. It is a government program that changes automatically depending on GDP and a person`s income, and acts as a negative feedback loop on GDP.

The size of the government deficit tends to increase as a country enters recession, which helps keep national income high through the multiplier.

Economic forecasting

Economic forecasting is the process of making predictions about the economy as a whole or in part.

Relevant models include

· Economic base analysis

· Shift-share analysis

· Input-output model

· Grinold and Kroner Model

.

Collective bargaining

Collective bargaining is a process between employers and employees to reach an agreement regarding the rights and duties of people at work. Collective bargaining aims to reach a collective agreement which usually sets out issues such as employees pay, working hours, training, health and safety, and rights to participate in workplace or company affairs.

During the bargaining process, employees are typically represented by a trade union.

Government debt

Government debt is money (or credit) owed by any level of government; either central government, federal government, municipal government or local government. By contrast, annual government deficit refers to the difference between government receipts and spending in a single year. Debt of a sovereign government is called sovereign debt.

Lucas critique

The Lucas critique argues that it is naive to try to predict the effects of a change in economic policy entirely on the basis of relationships observed in historical data, especially highly aggregated historical data.

The basic idea pre-dates Lucas` contribution (related ideas are expressed as Campbell`s Law and Goodhart`s Law), but in a 1976 paper Lucas drove home the point that this simple notion invalidated policy advice based on conclusions drawn from estimated system of equation models. Because the parameters of those models were not structural, i.e. not policy-invariant, they would necessarily change whenever policy (the rules of the game) was changed. Policy conclusions based on those models would therefore potentially be misleading. This argument called into question the prevailing large-scale econometric models that lacked foundations in dynamic economic theory.

Depression

In economics, a depression is a sustained, long-term downturn in economic activity in one or more economies. It is a more severe downturn than a recession, which is seen by economists as part of a normal business cycle.

Considered a rare and extreme form of recession, a depression is characterized by its length, and by abnormally large increases in unemployment, falls in the availability of credit-- quite often due to some kind of banking/financial crisis, shrinking output and investment, numerous bankruptcies-- including sovereign debt defaults, significantly reduced amounts of trade and commerce-- especially international, as well as highly volatile relative currency value fluctuations-- most often due to devaluations.

Great Depression

The Great Depression was a severe worldwide economic depression in the decade preceding World War II. The timing of the Great Depression varied across nations, but in most countries it started in about 1929 and lasted until the late 1930s or early 1940s. It was the longest, most widespread, and deepest depression of the 20th century, and is used in the 21st century as an example of how far the world`s economy can decline.

John Maynard Keynes

John Maynard Keynes, 1st Baron Keynes, CB was a British economist whose ideas have profoundly affected the theory and practice of modern macroeconomics, as well as the economic policies of governments. He identified the causes of business cycles, and advocated the use of fiscal and monetary measures to mitigate the adverse effects of economic recessions and depressions. His ideas are the basis for the school of thought known as Keynesian economics, and its various offshoots.

Money	Money is anything that is generally accepted as payment for goods and services and repayment of debts. The main functions of Money are distinguished as: a medium of exchange; a unit of account; a store of value; and, occasionally, a standard of deferred payment. Money originated as commodity Money, but nearly all contemporary Money systems are based on fiat Money.
Inflation	In economics, Inflation is a rise in the general level of prices of goods and services in an economy over a period of time. When the price level rises, each unit of currency buys fewer goods and services; consequently, annual Inflation is also an erosion in the purchasing power of money - a loss of real value in the internal medium of exchange and unit of account in the economy. A chief measure of price Inflation is the Inflation rate, the annualized percentage change in a general price index over time.
Stagflation	In economics, the term Stagflation refers to the situation when both the inflation rate and the unemployment rate are high. It is a difficult economic condition for a country, as both inflation and economic stagnation occur simultaneously and no macroeconomic policy can address both of these problems at the same time. The portmanteau Stagflation is generally attributed to British politician Iain Macleod, who coined the term in a speech to Parliament in 1965.
Business cycle	The term Business cycle refers to economy-wide fluctuations in production or economic activity over several months or years. These fluctuations occur around a long-term growth trend, and typically involve shifts over time between periods of relatively rapid economic growth (expansion or boom), and periods of relative stagnation or decline (contraction or recession). These fluctuations are often measured using the growth rate of real gross domestic product.
Discretionary policy	Discretionary policy is a term used to describe macroeconomic policy based on the ad hoc judgment of policymakers as opposed to policy set by predetermined rules. For instance, a central banker could make decisions on interest rates on a case by case basis instead of allowing a set rule, such as the Taylor rule, determine interest rates. Discretionary policies are similar to `feedback-rule policies` used by the Federal Reserve to achieve price level stability.

Central Bank

A Central bank, reserve bank, or monetary authority is a banking institution granted the exclusive privilege to lend a government its currency. Like a normal commercial bank, a Central bank charges interest on the loans made to borrowers, primarily the government of whichever country the bank exists for, and to other commercial banks, typically as a `lender of last resort`. However, a Central bank is distinguished from a normal commercial bank because it has a monopoly on creating the currency of that nation, which is loaned to the government in the form of legal tender.

Inflation targeting

Inflation targeting is an economic policy in which a central bank estimates and makes public a projected, or `target`, inflation rate and then attempts to steer actual inflation towards the target through the use of interest rate changes and other monetary tools.

Because interest rates and the inflation rate tend to be inversely related, the likely moves of the central bank to raise or lower interest rates become more transparent under the policy of Inflation targeting. Examples:

· if inflation appears to be above the target, the bank is likely to raise interest rates. This usually (but not always) has the effect over time of cooling the economy and bringing down inflation.

· if inflation appears to be below the target, the bank is likely to lower interest rates.

Monetary policy

Monetary policy is the process by which the central bank or monetary authority of a country controls the supply of money and the rate of interest. Monetary policy is usually used to attain a set of objectives oriented towards the growth and stability of the economy. These goals usually include stable prices and low unemployment.

Surplus

The term surplus is used in economics for several related quantities. The consumer surplus is the amount that consumers benefit by being able to purchase a product for a price that is less than the most that they would be willing to pay. The producer surplus is the amount that producers benefit by selling at a market price mechanism that is higher than the least that they would be willing to sell for.

Devaluation

Devaluation comes from the word `devalue`, which according to Merriam-Webster means `to lessen the value of.` As such, `Devaluation` is a reduction in the value of a currency with respect to those goods, services or other monetary units with which that currency can be exchanged.

In common modern usage, it specifically implies an official lowering of the value of a country`s currency within a fixed exchange rate system, by which the monetary authority formally sets a new fixed rate with respect to a foreign reference currency. In contrast, depreciation is used for the unofficial decrease in the exchange rate in a floating exchange rate system.

Exchange

An exchange is a highly organized market where (especially) tradable securities, commodities, foreign exchange, futures, and options contracts are sold and bought. exchanges bring together brokers and dealers who buy and sell these objects. These various financial instruments can typically be sold either through the exchange, typically with the benefit of a clearinghouse to cover defaults, or over-the-counter, where there is typically less protection against counterparty risk from clearinghouses although OTC clearinghouses have become more common over the years, with regulators placing pressure on the OTC markets to clear and display trades openly.

Exchange rate

In finance, the Exchange rates between two currencies specifies how much one currency is worth in terms of the other. It is the value of a foreign nation`s currency in terms of the home nation`s currency.

Aggregate Demand-Aggregate Supply model

Aggregate Demand-Aggregate Supply model is a macroeconomic model that explains price level and output through the relationship of aggregate demand and aggregate supply. It was first put forth by John Maynard Keynes in his work The General Theory of Employment, Interest, and Money. It is the foundation for the modern field of macroeconomics, and is accepted by a broad array of economists, from Libertarian, Monetarist supporters of laissez-faire, such as Milton Friedman to Socialist, Post-Keynesian supporters of economic interventionism, such as Joan Robinson.

Deflation

Deflation is a decrease in the general price level of goods and services. Deflation occurs when the annual inflation rate falls below zero percent (a negative inflation rate), resulting in an increase in the real value of money - allowing one to buy more goods with the same amount of money. This should not be confused with disinflation, a slow-down in the inflation rate.

Hyperinflation

Hyperinflation is inflation that is very high or `out of control`, a condition in which prices increase rapidly as a currency loses its value. Definitions used by the media vary from a cumulative inflation rate over three years approaching 100% to `inflation exceeding 50% a month.` In informal usage the term is often applied to much lower rates. As a rule of thumb, normal inflation is reported per year, but Hyperinflation is often reported for much shorter intervals, often per month.

Loss function

In statistics, decision theory and economics, a Loss function is a function that maps an event onto a real number representing the economic cost or regret associated with the event.

More specifically, in statistics a Loss function represents the loss (cost in money or loss in utility in some other sense) associated with an estimate being `wrong` (different from either a desired or a true value) as a function of a measure of the degree of wrongness (generally the difference between the estimated value and the true or desired value).

Given a random variable X over the probability space $(\mathcal{X},\Sigma,P_\theta)$ determined by a parameter $\theta \in \Theta$, and a set A of possible actions, a decision rule is a function $\delta : \mathcal{X} \rightarrow A$.

A Loss function is a real lower-bounded function L on $\Theta \times A$. The value $L(\theta, \delta)$ is the cost of action $\delta(X)$ under parameter θ.

Chapter 16. Government Debt and Budget Deficits

Government debt	Government debt is money (or credit) owed by any level of government; either central government, federal government, municipal government or local government. By contrast, annual government deficit refers to the difference between government receipts and spending in a single year. Debt of a sovereign government is called sovereign debt.
Budget deficit	A budget deficit occurs when an entity spends more money than it takes in. The opposite of a budget deficit is a budget surplus.
Balanced budget	A Balanced budget is when there is neither a budget deficit or a budget surplus - when revenues equal expenditure (\`the accounts balance\`) - particularly by a government. More generally, it refers to when there is no deficit, but possibly a surplus. A cyclically Balanced budget is a budget that is not necessarily balanced year-to-year, but is balanced over the economic cycle, running a surplus in boom years and running a deficit in lean years, with these offsetting over time.
Fiscal policy	In economics, Fiscal policy is the use of government expenditure and revenue collection to influence the economy. Fiscal policy can be contrasted with the other main type of macroeconomic policy, monetary policy, which attempts to stabilize the economy by controlling interest rates and the supply of money. The two main instruments of Fiscal policy are government expenditure and taxation. Changes in the level and composition of taxation and government spending can impact on the following variables in the economy: · Aggregate demand and the level of economic activity; · The pattern of resource allocation; · The distribution of income Fiscal policy refers to the use of the government budget to influence the first of these: economic activity.

Collective bargaining	Collective bargaining is a process between employers and employees to reach an agreement regarding the rights and duties of people at work. Collective bargaining aims to reach a collective agreement which usually sets out issues such as employees pay, working hours, training, health and safety, and rights to participate in workplace or company affairs. During the bargaining process, employees are typically represented by a trade union.
Economic growth	Economic growth is a term used to indicate the increase of per capita gross domestic product (GDP) or other measure of aggregate income. It is often measured as the rate of change in GDP. Economic growth refers only to the quantity of goods and services produced.
Exchange	An exchange is a highly organized market where (especially) tradable securities, commodities, foreign exchange, futures, and options contracts are sold and bought. exchanges bring together brokers and dealers who buy and sell these objects. These various financial instruments can typically be sold either through the exchange, typically with the benefit of a clearinghouse to cover defaults, or over-the-counter, where there is typically less protection against counterparty risk from clearinghouses although OTC clearinghouses have become more common over the years, with regulators placing pressure on the OTC markets to clear and display trades openly.
Exchange rate	In finance, the Exchange rates between two currencies specifies how much one currency is worth in terms of the other. It is the value of a foreign nation`s currency in terms of the home nation`s currency.
Income	Income is the consumption and savings opportunity gained by an entity within a specified time frame, which is generally expressed in monetary terms. However, for households and individuals, `Income is the sum of all the wages, salaries, profits, interests payments, rents and other forms of earnings received... in a given period of time.` For firms, Income generally refers to net-profit: what remains of revenue after expenses have been subtracted.
Population growth	In demography, Population growth is used informally for the more specific term Population growth rate , and is often used to refer specifically to the growth of the human population of the world. Simple models of Population growth include the Malthusian Growth Model and the logistic model.

In demographics and ecology, Population growth rate (PGR) is the fractional rate at which the number of individuals in a population increases.

Normal goods

In economics, Normal goods are any goods for which demand increases when income increases and falls when income decreases but price remains constant, i.e. with a positive income elasticity of demand. The term does not necessarily refer to the quality of the good.

Depending on the indifference curves, the amount of a good bought can either increase, decrease, or stay the same when income increases.

Investment

Investment is the commitment of money or capital to purchase financial instruments or other assets in order to gain profitable returns in form of interest, income, or appreciation of the value of the instrument. It is related to saving or deferring consumption. Investment is involved in many areas of the economy, such as business management and finance no matter for households, firms, or governments.

Security

A security is a fungible, negotiable instrument representing financial value. Securities are broadly categorized into debt securities (such as banknotes, bonds and debentures) and equity securities, e.g., common stocks; and derivative contracts, such as forwards, futures, options and swaps. The company or other entity issuing the security is called the issuer.

Social Security

Social security is primarily a social insurance program providing social protection, or protection against socially recognized conditions, including poverty, old age, disability, unemployment and others. Social security may refer to:

· social insurance, where people receive benefits or services in recognition of contributions to an insurance scheme. These services typically include provision for retirement pensions, disability insurance, survivor benefits and unemployment insurance.

· income maintenance--mainly the distribution of cash in the event of interruption of employment, including retirement, disability and unemployment

· services provided by administrations responsible for Social security. In different countries this may include medical care, aspects of social work and even industrial relations.

	· More rarely, the term is also used to refer to basic security, a term roughly equivalent to access to basic necessities--things such as food, clothing, shelter, education, money, and medical care.
Aggregate Demand-Aggregate Supply model	Aggregate Demand-Aggregate Supply model is a macroeconomic model that explains price level and output through the relationship of aggregate demand and aggregate supply. It was first put forth by John Maynard Keynes in his work The General Theory of Employment, Interest, and Money. It is the foundation for the modern field of macroeconomics, and is accepted by a broad array of economists, from Libertarian, Monetarist supporters of laissez-faire, such as Milton Friedman to Socialist, Post-Keynesian supporters of economic interventionism, such as Joan Robinson.
Deflation	Deflation is a decrease in the general price level of goods and services. Deflation occurs when the annual inflation rate falls below zero percent (a negative inflation rate), resulting in an increase in the real value of money - allowing one to buy more goods with the same amount of money. This should not be confused with disinflation, a slow-down in the inflation rate.
Hyperinflation	Hyperinflation is inflation that is very high or \`out of control\`, a condition in which prices increase rapidly as a currency loses its value. Definitions used by the media vary from a cumulative inflation rate over three years approaching 100% to \`inflation exceeding 50% a month.\` In informal usage the term is often applied to much lower rates. As a rule of thumb, normal inflation is reported per year, but Hyperinflation is often reported for much shorter intervals, often per month.
Capital	In economics, capital, capital goods, or real capital are factors of production used to create goods or services that are not themselves significantly consumed (though they may depreciate) in the production process. capital goods may be acquired with money or financial capital. In finance and accounting, capital generally refers to saved-up financial wealth, especially that used to start or maintain a business.
Capital asset	Capital asset refers to any asset used to make money, as opposed to assets used for personal enjoyment or consumption. This is an important distinction because two people can disagree sharply about the value of personal assets, one person might think a sports car is more valuable than a pickup truck, another person might have the opposite taste. But if an asset is held for the purpose of making money, taste has nothing to do with it, only differences of opinion about how much money the asset will produce.

Capital budgeting

Capital budgeting is the planning process used to determine whether a firm`s long term investments such as new machinery, replacement machinery, new plants, new products, and research development projects are worth pursuing. It is budget for major capital, or investment, expenditures.

Many formal methods are used in Capital budgeting, including the techniques such as

· Accounting rate of return

· Net present value

· Profitability index

· Internal rate of return

· Modified internal rate of return

· Equivalent annuity

These methods use the incremental cash flows from each potential investment, or project Techniques based on accounting earnings and accounting rules are sometimes used - though economists consider this to be improper - such as the accounting rate of return, and `return on investment.` Simplified and hybrid methods are used as well, such as payback period and discounted payback period.

Each potential project`s value should be estimated using a discounted cash flow (DCF) valuation, to find its net present value (NPV).

Recession

In economics, a Recession is a business cycle contraction, a general slowdown in economic activity over a period of time. During Recessions, many macroeconomic indicators vary in a similar way. Production as measured by Gross Domestic Product (GDP), employment, investment spending, capacity utilization, household incomes, business profits and inflation all fall during Recessions; while bankruptcies and the unemployment rate rise.

Financial crisis	The term Financial crisis is applied broadly to a variety of situations in which some financial institutions or assets suddenly lose a large part of their value. In the 19th and early 20th centuries, many financial crises were associated with banking panics, and many recessions coincided with these panics. Other situations that are often called financial crises include stock market crashes and the bursting of other financial bubbles, currency crises, and sovereign defaults.
Business cycle	The term Business cycle refers to economy-wide fluctuations in production or economic activity over several months or years. These fluctuations occur around a long-term growth trend, and typically involve shifts over time between periods of relatively rapid economic growth (expansion or boom), and periods of relative stagnation or decline (contraction or recession). These fluctuations are often measured using the growth rate of real gross domestic product.
Incentive	In economics and sociology, an Incentive is any factor (financial or non-financial) that enables or motivates a particular course of action, or counts as a reason for preferring one choice to the alternatives. It is an expectation that encourages people to behave in a certain way. Since human beings are purposeful creatures, the study of Incentive structures is central to the study of all economic activity (both in terms of individual decision-making and in terms of co-operation and competition within a larger institutional structure).
Tax cut	Economic stimulus via Tax cuts, along with interest rate intervention and deficit spending, are one of the central tenets of Keynesian economics. The immediate effects of a Tax cut are, generally, a decrease in the real income of the government and an increase in the real income of those whose tax rate has been lowered.
Money	Money is anything that is generally accepted as payment for goods and services and repayment of debts. The main functions of Money are distinguished as: a medium of exchange; a unit of account; a store of value; and, occasionally, a standard of deferred payment. Money originated as commodity Money, but nearly all contemporary Money systems are based on fiat Money.

Funding	Funding is to provide resources, usually in form of money (Financing), or other values such as effort or time (sweat equity), for a project, a person, a business or any other private or public institutions. When a request for Funding is made then fundraising is being attempted. Those funds can be allocated for either short term or long term purposes.
Principles of Political Economy	Principles of Political Economy by John Stuart Mill was the most important economics or political economy textbook of the mid nineteenth century. It was revised until its seventh edition in 1871, shortly before Mill`s death in 1873, and republished in numerous other editions.  Mill`s Principles were written in a style of prose far flung from the introductory texts of today.
Short-run	In economics, the concept of the Short-run refers to the decision-making time frame of a firm in which at least one factor of production is fixed. Costs which are fixed in the Short-run have no impact on a firm decisions. For example a firm can raise output by increasing the amount of labor through overtime. A generic firm can make three changes in the Short-run: · Increase production · Decrease production · Shut down In the Short-run, a profit maximizing firm will: · Increase production if marginal cost is less than price; · Decrease production if marginal cost is greater than price;

· Continue producing if average variable cost is less than price, even if average total cost is greater than price;

· Shut down if average variable cost is greater than price.

Aggregate supply

In economics, Aggregate supply is the total supply of goods and services that firms in a national economy plan on selling during a specific time period. It is the total amount of goods and services that firms are willing to sell at a given price level in an economy.

In neo-Keynesian theory seen in many textbooks, an `Aggregate supply and demand` diagram is drawn that looks like a typical Marshallian supply and demand diagram.

Monetary policy

Monetary policy is the process by which the central bank or monetary authority of a country controls the supply of money and the rate of interest. Monetary policy is usually used to attain a set of objectives oriented towards the growth and stability of the economy. These goals usually include stable prices and low unemployment.

Redistribution

In economics, redistribution is the transfer of income, wealth or property from some individuals to others. Most often it refers to progressive redistribution, from the rich to the poor, although it may also refer to regressive redistribution, from the poor to the rich. The desirability and effects of redistribution are actively debated on ethical and economic grounds.

Economic policy

Economic policy refers to the actions that governments take in the economic field. It covers the systems for setting interest rates and government budget as well as the labour market, national ownership, and many other areas of government interventions into the economy.

Such policies are often influenced by international institutions like the International Monetary Fund or World Bank as well as political beliefs and the consequent policies of parties.

Stagflation

In economics, the term Stagflation refers to the situation when both the inflation rate and the unemployment rate are high. It is a difficult economic condition for a country, as both inflation and economic stagnation occur simultaneously and no macroeconomic policy can address both of these problems at the same time.

The portmanteau Stagflation is generally attributed to British politician Iain Macleod, who coined the term in a speech to Parliament in 1965.

Bond	In finance, a bond is a debt security, in which the authorized issuer owes the holders a debt and, depending on the terms of the bond, is obliged to pay interest (the coupon) and/or to repay the principal at a later date, termed maturity. A bond is a formal contract to repay borrowed money with interest at fixed intervals. Thus a bond is like a loan: the issuer is the borrower (debtor), the holder is the lender (creditor), and the coupon is the interest.

Consumption	Consumption is a common concept in economics, and gives rise to derived concepts such as consumer debt. Generally, Consumption is defined in part by opposition to production. But the precise definition can vary because different schools of economists define production quite differently.
Average propensity to consume	Average propensity to consume is the percentage of income spent. To find the percentage of income spent, one needs to divide consumption by income, or $APC = \frac{C}{Y}$. In an economy in which each individual consumer saves lots of money, there is a tendency of people losing their jobs because demand for goods and services will be low.
Consumption function	In economics, the Consumption function is a single mathematical function used to express consumer spending. It was developed by John Maynard Keynes and detailed most famously in his book The General Theory of Employment, Interest, and Money. The function is used to calculate the amount of total consumption in an economy.
John Maynard Keynes	John Maynard Keynes, 1st Baron Keynes, CB was a British economist whose ideas have profoundly affected the theory and practice of modern macroeconomics, as well as the economic policies of governments. He identified the causes of business cycles, and advocated the use of fiscal and monetary measures to mitigate the adverse effects of economic recessions and depressions. His ideas are the basis for the school of thought known as Keynesian economics, and its various offshoots.
Money	Money is anything that is generally accepted as payment for goods and services and repayment of debts. The main functions of Money are distinguished as: a medium of exchange; a unit of account; a store of value; and, occasionally, a standard of deferred payment. Money originated as commodity Money, but nearly all contemporary Money systems are based on fiat Money.
Marginal propensity to consume	In economics, the Marginal propensity to consume is an empirical metric that quantifies induced consumption, the concept that the increase in personal consumer spending (consumption) that occurs with an increase in disposable income (income after taxes and transfers). For example, if a household earns one extra dollar of disposable income, and the Marginal propensity to consume is 0.65, then of that dollar, the household will spend 65 cents and save 35 cents.

Mathematically, the Marginal propensity to consume function is expressed as the derivative of the consumption (C) function with respect to disposable income (Y).

$$MPC = \frac{dC}{dY}$$

OR

$$MPC = \frac{\Delta C}{\Delta Y}$$

, where ΔC is the change in consumption, and ΔY is the change in disposable income that produced the consumption.

Economic stagnation

Economic stagnation is a prolonged period of slow economic growth (traditionally measured in terms of the GDP growth). Under some definitions, `slow` means significantly slower than potential growth as estimated by experts in macroeconomics. Under other definitions, growth less than 2-3% per year is a sign of stagnation.

Aggregate demand

In macroeconomics, Aggregate demand is the total demand for final goods and services in the economy (Y) at a given time and price level. It is the amount of goods and services in the economy that will be purchased at all possible price levels. This is the demand for the gross domestic product of a country when inventory levels are static.

Aggregate supply

In economics, Aggregate supply is the total supply of goods and services that firms in a national economy plan on selling during a specific time period. It is the total amount of goods and services that firms are willing to sell at a given price level in an economy.

In neo-Keynesian theory seen in many textbooks, an `Aggregate supply and demand` diagram is drawn that looks like a typical Marshallian supply and demand diagram.

Budget constraint

A Budget constraint represents the combinations of goods and services that a consumer can purchase given current prices with his or her income. Consumer theory uses the concepts of a Budget constraint and a preference map to analyze consumer choices. Both concepts have a ready graphical representation in the two-good case.

Time preference

In economics, Time preference pertains to how large a premium a consumer will place on enjoyment nearer in time over more remote enjoyment.

There is no absolute distinction that separates `high` and `low` Time preference, only comparisons with others either individually or in aggregate. Someone with a high Time preference is focused substantially on his well-being in the present and the immediate future relative to the average person, while someone with low Time preference places more emphasis than average on their well-being in the further future.

Present value

Present value is the value on a given date of a future payment or series of future payments, discounted to reflect the time value of money and other factors such as investment risk. Present value calculations are widely used in business and economics to provide a means to compare cash flows at different times on a meaningful `like to like` basis.

If offered a choice between $100 today or $100 in one year ceteris paribus, a rational person will choose $100 today.

Indifference curve

In microeconomic theory, an Indifference curve is a graph showing different bundles of goods, each measured as to quantity, between which a consumer is indifferent. That is, at each point on the curve, the consumer has no preference for one bundle over another. In other words, they are all equally preferred.

Marginal rate of substitution

In economics, the Marginal rate of substitution is the rate at which a consumer is ready to give up one good in exchange for another good while maintaining the same level of satisfaction.

Under the standard assumption of neoclassical economics that goods and services are continuously divisible, the marginal rates of substitution will be the same regardless of the direction of exchange, and will correspond to the slope of an indifference curve passing through the consumption bundle in question, at that point: mathematically, it is the implicit derivative. MRS of Y for X is the amount of Y for which a consumer is willing to exchange for X locally.

Economic indicator

An Economic indicator is a statistic about the economy. Economic indicators allow analysis of economic performance and predictions of future performance. One application of Economic indicators is the study of business cycles.

Chapter 17. Consumption

Standard of living	Standard of living is generally measured by standards such as real (i.e. inflation adjusted) income per person and poverty rate. Other measures such as access and quality of health care, income growth inequality and educational standards are also used. Examples are access to certain goods , or measures of health such as life expectancy.
Income	Income is the consumption and savings opportunity gained by an entity within a specified time frame, which is generally expressed in monetary terms. However, for households and individuals, `Income is the sum of all the wages, salaries, profits, interests payments, rents and other forms of earnings received... in a given period of time.` For firms, Income generally refers to net-profit: what remains of revenue after expenses have been subtracted.
Normal goods	In economics, Normal goods are any goods for which demand increases when income increases and falls when income decreases but price remains constant, i.e. with a positive income elasticity of demand. The term does not necessarily refer to the quality of the good. Depending on the indifference curves, the amount of a good bought can either increase, decrease, or stay the same when income increases.
Circular flow of income	In neoclassical economics, the terms Circular flow of income refer to a simple economic model which describes the reciprocal circulation of income between producers and consumers. In the circular flow model, the inter-dependent entities of producer and consumer are referred to as `firms` and `households` respectively and provide each other with factors in order to facilitate the flow of income. Firms provide consumers with goods and services in exchange for consumer expenditure and `factors of production` from households.
Consumption smoothing	Consumption smoothing is an economic concept which refers to balancing out spending and saving to attain and maintain the highest possible living standard over the course of one`s life. It is related to the permanent income hypothesis popularized by Milton Friedman and the Ramsey model of economic growth.
Real interest rate	The Real interest rate is approximately the nominal interest rate minus the inflation rate. It is the rate of interest an investor expects to receive after subtracting inflation. This is not a single number, as different investors have different expectations of future inflation. If, for example, an investor were able to lock in a 5% interest rate for the coming year and anticipated a 2% rise in prices, it would expect to earn a Real interest rate of 3%.
Liquidity constraint	A Liquidity constraint in economic theory is a form of imperfection in the capital market. It causes difficulties for models based on intertemporal consumption.

Many economic models require individuals to save or borrow money from time to time.

Intertemporal choice

Intertemporal choice is the study of the relative value people assign to two or more payoffs at different points in time. This relationship is usually simplified to today and some future date. Intertemporal choice was introduced by John Rae in 1834 in the `Sociological Theory of Capital`.

Exchange

An exchange is a highly organized market where (especially) tradable securities, commodities, foreign exchange, futures, and options contracts are sold and bought. exchanges bring together brokers and dealers who buy and sell these objects. These various financial instruments can typically be sold either through the exchange, typically with the benefit of a clearinghouse to cover defaults, or over-the-counter, where there is typically less protection against counterparty risk from clearinghouses although OTC clearinghouses have become more common over the years, with regulators placing pressure on the OTC markets to clear and display trades openly.

Exchange rate

In finance, the Exchange rates between two currencies specifies how much one currency is worth in terms of the other. It is the value of a foreign nation`s currency in terms of the home nation`s currency.

Security

A security is a fungible, negotiable instrument representing financial value. Securities are broadly categorized into debt securities (such as banknotes, bonds and debentures) and equity securities, e.g., common stocks; and derivative contracts, such as forwards, futures, options and swaps. The company or other entity issuing the security is called the issuer.

Social Security

Social security is primarily a social insurance program providing social protection, or protection against socially recognized conditions, including poverty, old age, disability, unemployment and others. Social security may refer to:

· social insurance, where people receive benefits or services in recognition of contributions to an insurance scheme. These services typically include provision for retirement pensions, disability insurance, survivor benefits and unemployment insurance.

· income maintenance--mainly the distribution of cash in the event of interruption of employment, including retirement, disability and unemployment

· services provided by administrations responsible for Social security. In different countries this may include medical care, aspects of social work and even industrial relations.

	· More rarely, the term is also used to refer to basic security, a term roughly equivalent to access to basic necessities--things such as food, clothing, shelter, education, money, and medical care.
Real gross domestic product	Real gross domestic product is a macroeconomic measure of the size of an economy adjusted for price changes Gross domestic product is defined as the market value of all final goods and services produced in a geographical region, usually a country. That market value depends on two things: the actual quantity of goods and services produced, and their price. The actual quantity of goods and services produced is sometimes called the volume.
Tax cut	Economic stimulus via Tax cuts, along with interest rate intervention and deficit spending, are one of the central tenets of Keynesian economics. The immediate effects of a Tax cut are, generally, a decrease in the real income of the government and an increase in the real income of those whose tax rate has been lowered.
Vietnam War	The Vietnam War was a Cold War military conflict that occurred in Vietnam, Laos, and Cambodia from November 1, 1955 , to April 30, 1975 when Saigon fell. This war followed the First Indochina War and was fought between the communist North Vietnam, supported by its communist allies, and the government of South Vietnam, supported by the United States and other anti-communist nations. The Viet Cong, a lightly-armed South Vietnamese communist-controlled common front, largely fought a guerrilla war against anti-communist forces in the region.
Collective bargaining	Collective bargaining is a process between employers and employees to reach an agreement regarding the rights and duties of people at work. Collective bargaining aims to reach a collective agreement which usually sets out issues such as employees pay, working hours, training, health and safety, and rights to participate in workplace or company affairs. During the bargaining process, employees are typically represented by a trade union.
Economic growth	Economic growth is a term used to indicate the increase of per capita gross domestic product (GDP) or other measure of aggregate income. It is often measured as the rate of change in GDP. Economic growth refers only to the quantity of goods and services produced.

Investment	Investment is the commitment of money or capital to purchase financial instruments or other assets in order to gain profitable returns in form of interest, income, or appreciation of the value of the instrument. It is related to saving or deferring consumption. Investment is involved in many areas of the economy, such as business management and finance no matter for households, firms, or governments.
Population growth	In demography, Population growth is used informally for the more specific term Population growth rate , and is often used to refer specifically to the growth of the human population of the world. Simple models of Population growth include the Malthusian Growth Model and the logistic model. In demographics and ecology, Population growth rate (PGR) is the fractional rate at which the number of individuals in a population increases.
Stagflation	In economics, the term Stagflation refers to the situation when both the inflation rate and the unemployment rate are high. It is a difficult economic condition for a country, as both inflation and economic stagnation occur simultaneously and no macroeconomic policy can address both of these problems at the same time. The portmanteau Stagflation is generally attributed to British politician Iain Macleod, who coined the term in a speech to Parliament in 1965.
Behavioral economics	Behavioral economics, and its related area of study behavioral finance, use social, cognitive and emotional factors in understanding the economic decisions of individuals and institutions performing economic functions, including consumers, borrowers and investors, and their effects on market prices, returns and the resource allocation. The fields are primarily concerned with the bounds of rationality (selfishness, self-control) of economic agents. Behavioral models typically integrate insights from psychology with neo-classical economic theory.
Financial crisis	The term Financial crisis is applied broadly to a variety of situations in which some financial institutions or assets suddenly lose a large part of their value. In the 19th and early 20th centuries, many financial crises were associated with banking panics, and many recessions coincided with these panics. Other situations that are often called financial crises include stock market crashes and the bursting of other financial bubbles, currency crises, and sovereign defaults.

Chapter 18. Investment

Inventory investment	Inventory investment is a component of gross domestic product (GDP). What is produced in a certain country is naturally also sold eventually, but some of the goods produced in a given year may be sold in a later year rather in the year they are produced. Conversely, some of the goods sold in a given year might have been produced in an earlier year.
Investment	Investment is the commitment of money or capital to purchase financial instruments or other assets in order to gain profitable returns in form of interest, income, or appreciation of the value of the instrument. It is related to saving or deferring consumption. Investment is involved in many areas of the economy, such as business management and finance no matter for households, firms, or governments.
Fixed investment	Fixed investment in economics refers to investment in fixed capital, i.e. tangible capital goods , or to the replacement of depreciated capital goods which have been scrapped. Thus, Fixed investment is investment in physical assets such as machinery, land, buildings, installations, vehicles, or technology. Normally, a company balance sheet will state both the amount of expenditure on fixed assets during the quarter or year, and the total value of the stock of fixed assets owned.
Capital	In economics, capital, capital goods, or real capital are factors of production used to create goods or services that are not themselves significantly consumed (though they may depreciate) in the production process. capital goods may be acquired with money or financial capital. In finance and accounting, capital generally refers to saved-up financial wealth, especially that used to start or maintain a business.
Cost	In business, retail, and accounting, a Cost is the value of money that has been used up to produce something, and hence is not available for use anymore. In economics, a Cost is an alternative that is given up as a result of a decision. In business, the Cost may be one of acquisition, in which case the amount of money expended to acquire it is counted as Cost.
Cost of capital	The Cost of capital is the cost of a company`s funds (both debt and equity), or, from an investor`s point of view `the expected return on a portfolio of all the company`s existing securities`. It is used to evaluate new projects of a company as it is the minimum return that investors expect for providing capital to the company, thus setting a benchmark that a new project has to meet.

	For an investment to be worthwhile, the expected return on capital must be greater than the Cost of capital.
Income	Income is the consumption and savings opportunity gained by an entity within a specified time frame, which is generally expressed in monetary terms. However, for households and individuals, `Income is the sum of all the wages, salaries, profits, interests payments, rents and other forms of earnings received... in a given period of time.` For firms, Income generally refers to net-profit: what remains of revenue after expenses have been subtracted.
Population growth	In demography, Population growth is used informally for the more specific term Population growth rate , and is often used to refer specifically to the growth of the human population of the world. Simple models of Population growth include the Malthusian Growth Model and the logistic model. In demographics and ecology, Population growth rate (PGR) is the fractional rate at which the number of individuals in a population increases.
Depreciation	Depreciation is a term used in accounting, economics and finance to spread the cost of an asset over the span of several years. In accounting, however, Depreciation is a term used to describe any method of attributing the historical or purchase cost of an asset across its useful life, roughly corresponding to normal wear and tear.
Inflation	In economics, Inflation is a rise in the general level of prices of goods and services in an economy over a period of time. When the price level rises, each unit of currency buys fewer goods and services; consequently, annual Inflation is also an erosion in the purchasing power of money - a loss of real value in the internal medium of exchange and unit of account in the economy. A chief measure of price Inflation is the Inflation rate, the annualized percentage change in a general price index over time.
Net investment	In economics, Net investment refers to an activity of spending which increases the availability of fixed capital goods or means of production. It is the total spending on new fixed investment minus replacement investment, which simply replaces depreciated capital goods.

Collective bargaining	Collective bargaining is a process between employers and employees to reach an agreement regarding the rights and duties of people at work. Collective bargaining aims to reach a collective agreement which usually sets out issues such as employees pay, working hours, training, health and safety, and rights to participate in workplace or company affairs. During the bargaining process, employees are typically represented by a trade union.
Determinant	In algebra, the Determinant is a special number associated with any square matrix. The fundamental geometric meaning of a Determinant is a scale factor for measure when the matrix is regarded as a linear transformation. Thus a 2 × 2 matrix with Determinant 2 when applied to a set of points with finite area will transform those points into a set with twice the area.
Exchange	An exchange is a highly organized market where (especially) tradable securities, commodities, foreign exchange, futures, and options contracts are sold and bought. exchanges bring together brokers and dealers who buy and sell these objects. These various financial instruments can typically be sold either through the exchange, typically with the benefit of a clearinghouse to cover defaults, or over-the-counter, where there is typically less protection against counterparty risk from clearinghouses although OTC clearinghouses have become more common over the years, with regulators placing pressure on the OTC markets to clear and display trades openly.
Exchange rate	In finance, the Exchange rates between two currencies specifies how much one currency is worth in terms of the other. It is the value of a foreign nation`s currency in terms of the home nation`s currency.
Government debt	Government debt is money (or credit) owed by any level of government; either central government, federal government, municipal government or local government. By contrast, annual government deficit refers to the difference between government receipts and spending in a single year. Debt of a sovereign government is called sovereign debt.
Income tax	An Income tax is a tax levied on the income of individuals or businesses (corporations or other legal entities). Various Income tax systems exist, with varying degrees of tax incidence. Income taxation can be progressive, proportional, or regressive.
Stock	The Stock or capital Stock of a business entity represents the original capital paid into or invested in the business by its founders. It serves as a security for the creditors of a business since it cannot be withdrawn to the detriment of the creditors. Stock is distinct from the property and the assets of a business which may fluctuate in quantity and value.

Stock market

A Stock market or equity market is a public market for the trading of company stock and derivatives at an agreed price; these are securities listed on a stock exchange as well as those only traded privately.

The size of the world Stock market was estimated at about $36.6 trillion US at the beginning of October 2008. The total world derivatives market has been estimated at about $791 trillion face or nominal value, 11 times the size of the entire world economy. The value of the derivatives market, because it is stated in terms of notional values, cannot be directly compared to a stock or a fixed income security, which traditionally refers to an actual value.

Tax Reform Act of 1986

The U.S. Congress passed the Tax Reform Act of 1986 (Pub.L. 99-514, 100 Stat. 2085, enacted October 22, 1986) to simplify the income tax code, broaden the tax base and eliminate many tax shelters and other preferences. Referred to as the second of the two `Reagan tax cuts` (the Kemp-Roth Tax Cut of 1981 being the first), the bill was also officially sponsored by Democrats, Richard Gephardt of Missouri in the House of Representatives and Bill Bradley of New Jersey in the Senate.

The tax reform was designed to be revenue neutral, but because individual taxes were decreased while corporate taxes were increased, Congressional Budget Office estimates (which ignore corporate taxes) suggested every tax payer saw a decrease in their tax bill.

James Tobin

James Tobin was an American economist who in his lifetime, had served on the Council of Economic Advisors, the Board of Governors of the Federal Reserve System, and had taught at Harvard and Yale Universities. He developed the ideas of Keynesian economics, and advocated government intervention to stabilize output and avoid recessions. His academic work included pioneering contributions to the study of investment, monetary and fiscal policy and financial markets.

Tax credits

Tax credits may be granted for various types of taxes in recognition of taxes already paid, as a subsidy, or to encourage investment or other behaviors. Tax credits may or may not be refundable to the extent they exceed the respective tax. Tax systems may grant Tax credits to businesses or individuals, and such grants vary by type of credit.

Economic indicator

An Economic indicator is a statistic about the economy. Economic indicators allow analysis of economic performance and predictions of future performance. One application of Economic indicators is the study of business cycles.

Recession

In economics, a Recession is a business cycle contraction, a general slowdown in economic activity over a period of time. During Recessions, many macroeconomic indicators vary in a similar way. Production as measured by Gross Domestic Product (GDP), employment, investment spending, capacity utilization, household incomes, business profits and inflation all fall during Recessions; while bankruptcies and the unemployment rate rise.

John Maynard Keynes

John Maynard Keynes, 1st Baron Keynes, CB was a British economist whose ideas have profoundly affected the theory and practice of modern macroeconomics, as well as the economic policies of governments. He identified the causes of business cycles, and advocated the use of fiscal and monetary measures to mitigate the adverse effects of economic recessions and depressions. His ideas are the basis for the school of thought known as Keynesian economics, and its various offshoots.

Speculation

In finance, Speculation is a financial action that does not promise safety of the initial investment along with the return on the principal sum. Speculation typically involves the lending of money or the purchase of assets, equity or debt but in a manner that has not been given thorough analysis or is deemed to have low margin of safety or a significant risk of the loss of the principal investment. The term, `Speculation,` which is formally defined as above in Graham and Dodd`s 1934 text, Security Analysis, contrasts with the term `investment,` which is a financial operation that, upon thorough analysis, promises safety of principal and a satisfactory return.

Business cycle

The term Business cycle refers to economy-wide fluctuations in production or economic activity over several months or years. These fluctuations occur around a long-term growth trend, and typically involve shifts over time between periods of relatively rapid economic growth (expansion or boom), and periods of relative stagnation or decline (contraction or recession).

These fluctuations are often measured using the growth rate of real gross domestic product.

Credit crunch

A Credit crunch is a reduction in the general availability of loans (or credit) or a sudden tightening of the conditions required to obtain a loan from the banks. A Credit crunch generally involves a reduction in the availability of credit independent of a rise in official interest rates. In such situations, the relationship between credit availability and interest rates has implicitly changed, such that either credit becomes less available at any given official interest rate, or there ceases to be a clear relationship between interest rates and credit availability (i.e.

Depression

In economics, a depression is a sustained, long-term downturn in economic activity in one or more economies. It is a more severe downturn than a recession, which is seen by economists as part of a normal business cycle.

	Considered a rare and extreme form of recession, a depression is characterized by its length, and by abnormally large increases in unemployment, falls in the availability of credit-- quite often due to some kind of banking/financial crisis, shrinking output and investment, numerous bankruptcies-- including sovereign debt defaults, significantly reduced amounts of trade and commerce-- especially international, as well as highly volatile relative currency value fluctuations-- most often due to devaluations.
Great Depression	The Great Depression was a severe worldwide economic depression in the decade preceding World War II. The timing of the Great Depression varied across nations, but in most countries it started in about 1929 and lasted until the late 1930s or early 1940s. It was the longest, most widespread, and deepest depression of the 20th century, and is used in the 21st century as an example of how far the world`s economy can decline.
Aggregate demand	In macroeconomics, Aggregate demand is the total demand for final goods and services in the economy (Y) at a given time and price level. It is the amount of goods and services in the economy that will be purchased at all possible price levels. This is the demand for the gross domestic product of a country when inventory levels are static.
Bank failure	A Bank failure occurs when a bank is unable to meet its obligations to its depositors or other creditors because it has become insolvent or too illiquid to meet its liabilities. More specifically, a bank usually fails economically when the market value of its assets declines to a value that is less than the market value of its liabilities. As such, the bank is unable to fulfill the demands of all of its depositors on time.
Economic growth	Economic growth is a term used to indicate the increase of per capita gross domestic product (GDP) or other measure of aggregate income. It is often measured as the rate of change in GDP. Economic growth refers only to the quantity of goods and services produced.
Financial crisis	The term Financial crisis is applied broadly to a variety of situations in which some financial institutions or assets suddenly lose a large part of their value. In the 19th and early 20th centuries, many financial crises were associated with banking panics, and many recessions coincided with these panics. Other situations that are often called financial crises include stock market crashes and the bursting of other financial bubbles, currency crises, and sovereign defaults.
Money	Money is anything that is generally accepted as payment for goods and services and repayment of debts. The main functions of Money are distinguished as: a medium of exchange; a unit of account; a store of value; and, occasionally, a standard of deferred payment.

	Money originated as commodity Money, but nearly all contemporary Money systems are based on fiat Money.
Stagflation	In economics, the term Stagflation refers to the situation when both the inflation rate and the unemployment rate are high. It is a difficult economic condition for a country, as both inflation and economic stagnation occur simultaneously and no macroeconomic policy can address both of these problems at the same time. The portmanteau Stagflation is generally attributed to British politician Iain Macleod, who coined the term in a speech to Parliament in 1965.
Aggregate Demand-Aggregate Supply model	Aggregate Demand-Aggregate Supply model is a macroeconomic model that explains price level and output through the relationship of aggregate demand and aggregate supply. It was first put forth by John Maynard Keynes in his work The General Theory of Employment, Interest, and Money. It is the foundation for the modern field of macroeconomics, and is accepted by a broad array of economists, from Libertarian, Monetarist supporters of laissez-faire, such as Milton Friedman to Socialist, Post-Keynesian supporters of economic interventionism, such as Joan Robinson.
Demand	In economics, demand is the desire to own anything and the ability to pay for it and willingness to pay . The term demand signifies the ability or the willingness to buy a particular commodity at a given point of time. Economists record demand on a demand schedule and plot it on a graph as a demand curve that is usually downward sloping.
Interest rate	An Interest rate is the price a borrower pays for the use of money they borrow from a lender, for instance a small company might borrow capital from a bank to buy new assets for their business, and the return a lender receives for deferring the use of funds, by lending it to the borrower. Interests rates are fundamental to a capitalist society. Interest rates are normally expressed as a percentage rate over the period of one year.
Structural unemployment	Structural unemployment is a form of unemployment resulting from a mismatch between the sufficiently skilled workers seeking employment and demand in the labour market. Even though the number of vacancies may be equal to the number of the unemployed, the unemployed workers may lack the skills needed for the jobs -- or may not live in the part of the country or world where the jobs are available.

	Structural unemployment is a result of the dynamics of the labor market and the fact that these can never be as flexible as, e.g., financial markets.
Factors of production	In economics, Factors of production are the resources employed to produce goods and services. They facilitate production but do not become part of the product (as with raw materials) or become significantly transformed by the production process . To 19th century economists, the Factors of production were land (natural resources, gifts from nature), labor (the ability to work), capital goods (human-made tools and equipment) and enterprise.
Real interest rate	The Real interest rate is approximately the nominal interest rate minus the inflation rate. It is the rate of interest an investor expects to receive after subtracting inflation. This is not a single number, as different investors have different expectations of future inflation. If, for example, an investor were able to lock in a 5% interest rate for the coming year and anticipated a 2% rise in prices, it would expect to earn a Real interest rate of 3%.

Chapter 19. Money Supply, Money Demand, and the Banking System

Money	Money is anything that is generally accepted as payment for goods and services and repayment of debts. The main functions of Money are distinguished as: a medium of exchange; a unit of account; a store of value; and, occasionally, a standard of deferred payment. Money originated as commodity Money, but nearly all contemporary Money systems are based on fiat Money.
Money supply	In economics, Money supply is the total amount of money available in an economy at a particular point in time. There are several ways to define `money,` but standard measures usually include currency in circulation and demand deposits. Money supply data are recorded and published, usually by the government or the central bank of the country. Public and private-sector analysts have long monitored changes in Money supply because of its possible effects on the price level, inflation and the business cycle.
Balance sheet	In financial accounting, a Balance sheet or statement of financial position is a summary of the financial balances of a sole proprietorship, a business partnership or a company. Assets, liabilities and ownership equity are listed as of a specific date, such as the end of its financial year. A Balance sheet is often described as a `snapshot of a company`s financial condition`.
Fractional-reserve banking	Fractional-reserve banking is the banking practice in which banks keep only a fraction of their deposits in reserve (as cash and other highly liquid assets) and lend out the remainder, while maintaining the simultaneous obligation to redeem all these deposits upon demand. Fractional reserve banking necessarily occurs when banks lend out any fraction of the funds received from deposit accounts, and is practiced by all modern commercial banks. By its nature, the practice of fractional reserve banking expands the money supply (cash and demand deposits) beyond what it would otherwise be.
Monetary policy	Monetary policy is the process by which the central bank or monetary authority of a country controls the supply of money and the rate of interest. Monetary policy is usually used to attain a set of objectives oriented towards the growth and stability of the economy. These goals usually include stable prices and low unemployment.

Bank failure	A Bank failure occurs when a bank is unable to meet its obligations to its depositors or other creditors because it has become insolvent or too illiquid to meet its liabilities. More specifically, a bank usually fails economically when the market value of its assets declines to a value that is less than the market value of its liabilities. As such, the bank is unable to fulfill the demands of all of its depositors on time.
Financial intermediary	A Financial intermediary is an entity that connects surplus and deficit agents. The classic example of a Financial intermediary is a bank that transforms bank deposits into bank loans. Through the process of financial intermediation, certain assets or liabilities are transformed into different assets or liabilities.
Monetary base	Monetary base is a term relating to the money supply (or money stock), the amount of money in the economy. The Monetary base is highly liquid money that consists of coins, paper money , and commercial banks\` reserves with the central bank. Measures of money are typically classified as levels of M, where the Monetary base is smallest and lowest M-level: M0. Base money can be described as the most acceptable form of final payment. Broader measures of the money supply also include money that does not count as base money, such as demand deposits (included in M1), and other deposit accounts like the less liquid savings accounts (included in M2) etc.
Money multiplier	A Money multiplier is one of various closely related ratios of commercial bank money to central bank money under a fractional-reserve banking system. Most often, it measures the maximum amount of commercial bank money that can be created by a given unit of central bank money. That is, in a fractional-reserve banking system, the total amount of loans that commercial banks are allowed to extend (the commercial bank money that they can legally create) is a multiple of reserves; this multiple is the reciprocal of the reserve ratio, and it is an economic multiplier.
Multiplier	In economics, the multiplier effect or spending multiplier is the idea that an initial amount of spending (usually by the government) leads to increased consumption spending and so results in an increase in national income greater than the initial amount of spending. In other words, an initial change in aggregate demand causes a change in aggregate output for the economy that is a multiple of the initial change. However, multiplier values less than one have been empirically measured, suggesting that certain types of government spending crowd out private investments and spending that would have otherwise happened.

Aggregate Demand-Aggregate Supply model	Aggregate Demand-Aggregate Supply model is a macroeconomic model that explains price level and output through the relationship of aggregate demand and aggregate supply. It was first put forth by John Maynard Keynes in his work The General Theory of Employment, Interest, and Money. It is the foundation for the modern field of macroeconomics, and is accepted by a broad array of economists, from Libertarian, Monetarist supporters of laissez-faire, such as Milton Friedman to Socialist, Post-Keynesian supporters of economic interventionism, such as Joan Robinson.
Exchange	An exchange is a highly organized market where (especially) tradable securities, commodities, foreign exchange, futures, and options contracts are sold and bought. exchanges bring together brokers and dealers who buy and sell these objects. These various financial instruments can typically be sold either through the exchange, typically with the benefit of a clearinghouse to cover defaults, or over-the-counter, where there is typically less protection against counterparty risk from clearinghouses although OTC clearinghouses have become more common over the years, with regulators placing pressure on the OTC markets to clear and display trades openly.
Exchange rate	In finance, the Exchange rates between two currencies specifies how much one currency is worth in terms of the other. It is the value of a foreign nation`s currency in terms of the home nation`s currency.
Mundell-Fleming model	The Mundell-Fleming model is an economic model first set forth by Robert Mundell and Marcus Fleming. The model is an extension of the IS-LM model. Whereas the traditional IS-LM Model deals with economy under autarky (or a closed economy), the Mundell-Fleming model tries to describe an open economy.
Reserve requirements	The Reserve requirements is a state bank regulation that sets the minimum reserves each bank must hold to customer deposits and notes. It would normally be in the form of fiat currency stored in a bank vault (vault cash), or with a central bank.
Capital	In economics, capital, capital goods, or real capital are factors of production used to create goods or services that are not themselves significantly consumed (though they may depreciate) in the production process. capital goods may be acquired with money or financial capital. In finance and accounting, capital generally refers to saved-up financial wealth, especially that used to start or maintain a business.

Good

In economics and accounting, a good is physical product that can be used to satisfy some desire or need. It can be contrasted with a service which is intangible, whereas a good is a tangible physical product, capable of being delivered to a purchaser and involves the transfer of ownership from seller to customer. For example, an apple is a tangible good, as opposed to a haircut, which is an (intangible) service.

Discount rate

The Discount rate is an interest rate a central bank charges depository institutions that borrow reserves from it.

The term Discount rate has two meanings:

· the same as interest rate; the term `discount` does not refer to the common meaning of the word, but to the meaning in computations of present value, e.g. net present value or discounted cash flow

· the annual effective Discount rate, which is the annual interest divided by the capital including that interest; this rate is lower than the interest rate; it corresponds to using the value after a year as the nominal value, and seeing the initial value as the nominal value minus a discount; it is used for Treasury Bills and similar financial instruments

The annual effective Discount rate is the annual interest divided by the capital including that interest, which is the interest rate divided by 100% plus the interest rate. It is the annual discount factor to be applied to the future cash flow, to find the discount, subtracted from a future value to find the value one year earlier.

For example, suppose there is a government bond that sells for $95 and pays $100 in a year`s time.

Excess reserves

Excess reserves are bank reserves in excess of the reserve requirement set by a central bank. They are reserves of cash more than the required amounts. Holding Excess reserves is generally considered costly and uneconomical as no interest is earned on the excess amount.

Central Bank

A Central bank, reserve bank, or monetary authority is a banking institution granted the exclusive privilege to lend a government its currency. Like a normal commercial bank, a Central bank charges interest on the loans made to borrowers, primarily the government of whichever country the bank exists for, and to other commercial banks, typically as a `lender of last resort`. However, a Central bank is distinguished from a normal commercial bank because it has a monopoly on creating the currency of that nation, which is loaned to the government in the form of legal tender.

Deposit Insurance

Explicit Deposit insurance is a measure implemented in many countries to protect bank depositors, in full or in part, from losses caused by a bank`s inability to pay its debts when due. Deposit insurance systems are one component of a financial system safety net that promotes financial stability.

Banks are allowed to lend or invest most of the money deposited with them instead of safe-keeping the full amounts .

Lender of last resort

A Lender of last resort is an institution willing to extend credit when no one else will. Originally the term referred to a reserve financial institution, most often the central bank of a country, that secured well-connected banks and other institutions that are too-big-to-fail against bankruptcy.

Due to fractional reserve banking, in aggregate, all lenders and borrowers are insolvent.

Capital requirement

The Capital requirement is a bank regulation, which sets a framework on how banks and depository institutions must handle their capital. The categorization of assets and capital is highly standardized so that it can be risk weighted . Internationally, the Basel Committee on Banking Supervision housed at the Bank for International Settlements influence each country`s banking Capital requirements.

Export-oriented industrialization	Export-oriented industrialization is a trade and economic policy aiming to speed-up the industrialization process of a country through exporting goods for which the nation has a comparative advantage. Export-led growth implies opening domestic markets to foreign competition in exchange for market access in other countries, though this may not be true of all domestic markets as governments aim to protect specific nascent industries so they grow and are able to exploit their future comparative advantage and in practise the converse can occur, for example many East Asian countries had strong barriers on imports during most of the 1960s-1980s. Reduced tariff barriers, floating exchange rate (devaluation of national currency is often employed to facilitate exports), and government support for exporting sectors are all an example of policies adopted to promote Export oriented industrialization, and ultimately economic development.
Federal Reserve System	The Federal Reserve System is the central banking system of the United States. It was created in 1913 with the enactment of the Federal Reserve Act, and was largely a response to a series of financial panics, particularly a severe panic in 1907. Over time, the roles and responsibilities of the Federal Reserve System have expanded and its structure has evolved.
Federal Reserve Bank	The twelve Federal Reserve Banks form a major part of the Federal Reserve System, the central banking system of the United States. The twelve Federal Reserve Banks together divide the nation into twelve Federal Reserve Districts, the the twelve banking districts created by the Federal Reserve Act of 1913. Each Federal Reserve Bank is responsible for the regulation of the commercial banks within its own particular district.
Leverage	In finance, leverage refers to the use of debt capital to supplement equity capital. Companies usually leverage to attempt to increase returns on equity capital, as it can increase the scope for gains or losses. The temporary increases in stock prices due to leverage at some banks in the United States have been blamed for the unusually high overall remuneration for top executives during the financial crisis of 2007-2010, since gains in stock prices were often rewarded regardless of how they were achieved.
Bond	In finance, a bond is a debt security, in which the authorized issuer owes the holders a debt and, depending on the terms of the bond, is obliged to pay interest (the coupon) and/or to repay the principal at a later date, termed maturity. A bond is a formal contract to repay borrowed money with interest at fixed intervals. Thus a bond is like a loan: the issuer is the borrower (debtor), the holder is the lender (creditor), and the coupon is the interest.

Demand

In economics, demand is the desire to own anything and the ability to pay for it and willingness to pay . The term demand signifies the ability or the willingness to buy a particular commodity at a given point of time.

Economists record demand on a demand schedule and plot it on a graph as a demand curve that is usually downward sloping.

Asset

In financial accounting, Assets are economic resources. Anything tangible or intangible that is capable of being owned or controlled to produce value and that is held to have positive economic value is considered an Asset. Simplistically stated, Assets represent ownership of value that can be converted into cash (although cash itself is also considered an Asset).

Portfolio

In finance, a portfolio is an appropriate mix or collection of investments held by an institution or an individual.

Holding a portfolio is a part of an investment and risk-limiting strategy called diversification. By owning several assets, certain types of risk can be reduced.

Cash management

In United States banking, Cash management is a marketing term for certain services offered primarily to larger business customers. It may be used to describe all bank accounts (such as checking accounts) provided to businesses of a certain size, but it is more often used to describe specific services such as cash concentration, zero balance accounting, and automated clearing house facilities. Sometimes, private banking customers are given Cash management services.

Financial innovation

Financial innovation refers to the creating and marketing of new types of securities.

Demise

Demise is an Anglo-Norman legal term for a transfer of an estate, especially by lease. The word has an operative effect in a lease implying a covenant `for quiet enjoyment`.

The phrase `Demise of the crown` is used in English law to signify the immediate transfer of the sovereignty, with all its attributes and prerogatives, to the successor without any interregnum in accordance with the maxim `the king never dies`.

Investment

Investment is the commitment of money or capital to purchase financial instruments or other assets in order to gain profitable returns in form of interest, income, or appreciation of the value of the instrument. It is related to saving or deferring consumption. Investment is involved in many areas of the economy, such as business management and finance no matter for households, firms, or governments.

Near Money

Near money is a term used in economics to describe highly liquid assets that can easily be converted into cash.

Various sources provide the following examples of Near money:

· Savings account

· Money funds

· Bank time deposits (Certificates of deposit)

· Government treasury securities (such as T-bills)

· Bonds near their redemption date

· Foreign currencies, especially widely traded ones such as the US dollar, euro or yen.

· list of countries by stocks of quasi money.

Macroeconomics

Macroeconomics is a branch of economics that deals with the performance, structure, behavior and decision-making of the entire economy, be that a national, regional, or the global economy. Along with microeconomics, Macroeconomics is one of the two most general fields in economics.

Macroeconomists study aggregated indicators such as GDP, unemployment rates, and price indices to understand how the whole economy functions.

Aggregate demand	In macroeconomics, Aggregate demand is the total demand for final goods and services in the economy (Y) at a given time and price level. It is the amount of goods and services in the economy that will be purchased at all possible price levels. This is the demand for the gross domestic product of a country when inventory levels are static.
Goods and services	In economics, economic output is divided into physical goods and intangible services. Consumption of Goods and services is assumed to produce utility. It is often used when referring to a Goods and services Tax.
Gross domestic product	The Gross domestic product or gross domestic income (GDI) is a measure of a country`s overall economic output. It is the market value of all final goods and services made within the borders of a country in a year. It is often positively correlated with the standard of living,; though its use as a stand-in for measuring the standard of living has come under increasing criticism and many countries are actively exploring alternative measures to Gross domestic product for that purpose.
Standard of living	Standard of living is generally measured by standards such as real (i.e. inflation adjusted) income per person and poverty rate. Other measures such as access and quality of health care, income growth inequality and educational standards are also used. Examples are access to certain goods , or measures of health such as life expectancy.
Deflation	Deflation is a decrease in the general price level of goods and services. Deflation occurs when the annual inflation rate falls below zero percent (a negative inflation rate), resulting in an increase in the real value of money - allowing one to buy more goods with the same amount of money. This should not be confused with disinflation, a slow-down in the inflation rate.
Hyperinflation	Hyperinflation is inflation that is very high or `out of control`, a condition in which prices increase rapidly as a currency loses its value. Definitions used by the media vary from a cumulative inflation rate over three years approaching 100% to `inflation exceeding 50% a month.` In informal usage the term is often applied to much lower rates. As a rule of thumb, normal inflation is reported per year, but Hyperinflation is often reported for much shorter intervals, often per month.
Phillips curve	In economics, the Phillips curve is a historical inverse relationship between the rate of unemployment and the rate of inflation in an economy. Stated simply, the lower the unemployment in an economy, the higher the rate of increase in nominal wages. While it has been observed that there is a stable short run tradeoff between unemployment and inflation this has not been observed in the long run.

Stabilization policy

A stabilization policy is a package or set of measures introduced to stabilize a financial system or economy. The term can refer to policies in two distinct sets of circumstances: business cycle stabilization and crisis stabilization.

Cost

In business, retail, and accounting, a Cost is the value of money that has been used up to produce something, and hence is not available for use anymore. In economics, a Cost is an alternative that is given up as a result of a decision. In business, the Cost may be one of acquisition, in which case the amount of money expended to acquire it is counted as Cost.

Cost of capital

The Cost of capital is the cost of a company`s funds (both debt and equity), or, from an investor`s point of view `the expected return on a portfolio of all the company`s existing securities`. It is used to evaluate new projects of a company as it is the minimum return that investors expect for providing capital to the company, thus setting a benchmark that a new project has to meet.

For an investment to be worthwhile, the expected return on capital must be greater than the Cost of capital.

Government debt

Government debt is money (or credit) owed by any level of government; either central government, federal government, municipal government or local government. By contrast, annual government deficit refers to the difference between government receipts and spending in a single year. Debt of a sovereign government is called sovereign debt.

CPSIA information can be obtained at www.ICGtesting.com
Printed in the USA
267443BV00001B/88/P

9 781617 446405